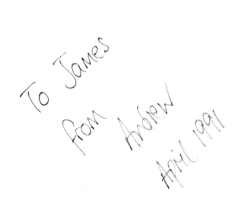

To James
From Andrew
April 1991

THE CRICKET MATCH

THE CRICKET MATCH

HUGH DE SELINCOURT

Illustrations by
PAUL COX

Stanley Paul

London   Sydney   Auckland   Johannesburg

STANLEY PAUL & CO. LTD
An imprint of Random Century Group Ltd
20 Vauxhall Bridge Road, London SW1V 2SA

Random Century Australia (Pty) Ltd
20 Alfred Street, Milsons Point, Sydney 2061

Random Century New Zealand Limited
PO Box 40-086, Glenfield, Auckland 10

Century Hutchinson South Africa (Pty) Ltd
PO Box 337, Bergvlei 2012, South Africa

Produced by Pilot Productions Ltd, London, England
Typeset by Dorchester Typesetting, Dorchester, England
Printed by Tien Wah Press (Pty) Ltd, Singapore

A CIP catalogue record for this book is
available from the British Library

ISBN: 0 09 174628 0

Copyright © Pilot Productions Ltd
Text copyright © Hugh de Selincourt

CONTENTS

TO

Frank W. Carter

in memory of many good games
watched and played together,
you in your small corner,
I in mine

MCMXXIV

EDITOR'S NOTE

In an early edition of *The Cricket Match*, which was first published in 1924, its editor wrote, 'Cricket is the one and only outdoor game which has remained purely English. Today, in nearly every other field of sport, foreign countries compete with us – often very successfully. But cricket is played by the British alone.'

Some might argue that the game of English cricket is even now played only in England, even only at village level, and that the game that is played elsewhere is something rather different.

What is certain is that the game that Hugh de Selincourt describes, while being quite recognisably cricket, is perceived also as a rich seam of English rural culture, a touchstone in a fast-changing modern world, even something of a social panacea.

The Cricket Match is not some clever intellectual exercise, however, it is real, born of the author's own experience. An empirical nature was at least one characteristic which de Selincourt shared with the Tillingfold Captain, Paul Gauvinier, and it stands him in good stead.

The sights, the sounds, the smells that the author describes all blur into a misty reminiscence of how things go on a sunny, summer afternoon of village cricket. And while the carefully observed characters may have been deliberately fashioned to suit his tale there is little doubt that many if not all were inspired by real acquaintances.

Knowing that the author had, for seven years, been Captain of Storrington Village Cricket Club, and that Storrington shares certain physical geographical features with the fictional Tillingfold, an excursion to West Sussex was inevitable.

Upon our arrival the illustrator, Paul Cox, and I went first to the village pub – alas, not 'The Dog and Duck' but very probably 'the pub at the end of the village' that Gauvinier preferred. There seemed nothing surprising in the barman's confession that he happened to be Vice Captain of SCC, nor in the implicitly trusting nature that freed him to hand over the keys of the Pavilion to a complete stranger.

Of course Storrington has changed in the sixty-five years since de Selincourt wrote his book, but it wasn't difficult to strip away the modifications and pick out the village of his day. Little has been removed, though it appears that over the years the inhabitants have pursued a single-minded policy of 'in-filling' (a tradition which continues to be observed almost obsessively today).

As we picked our way through the building sites towards the Recreation Ground, Paul was able to sketch many locations whose actuality fitted precisely their descriptions in the book.

In the churchyard I fell into conversation with a man who insisted on introducing me to an elderly relative who had an oil painting, a faithful likeness of the ground as it had been earlier this century and which in fact, as I discovered on seeing it, was also a replica of the Recreation Ground at Tillingfold.

On reaching the real cricket ground we met Stan Welland. There was a moment in our encounter when I nearly called him Hodgkiss, after the old timer in *The Cricket Match*, but perhaps the images he re-created for us carried rather the enthusiasm of a Horace Cairie. Stan had played for Storrington before some of the legendary characters mythologised by de Selincourt had passed on, and unprompted he shared with us reminiscences which themselves would not have seemed out of place in de Selincourt's original.

Stan Welland takes his cricket seriously, albeit now as a spectator. He is the most senior member of a club whose history stretches back to 1793, and he leaves you in no doubt that he makes his opinions heard. One senses in him just that loyalty and club identity that was, and in some places still is, the lifeblood of village cricket.

The tradition grew in an era when England was largely a patchwork of villages whose inhabitants were born, lived and died there, and rarely travelled far. Then, a man had loyalties not merely to a nation but to a particular part of his country. In that context cricket was a local cultural celebration, and for the players an opportunity to imbibe in 'the great refreshment that comes to mortals who forget themselves and join in a common purpose.'

Chapter One

THE VILLAGE OF TILLINGFOLD

Tillingfold lies in a hollow under the Downs, and climbs up the sides of the hill, like a pool risen to overflow its banks. The main street branches off in fingers up the sudden dip from the flat stretch that seemed, as you approached, to reach the foot of the Downs.

This unexpected stretch of rising country, on either side of the village, had been covered by miles of tall fir trees; but a keen business man bought the estate at the right moment during the war, and with the help of German prisoners had levelled all the fir trees, which were sawn into pit-props; soon afterwards, having resold the estate, he tactfully withdrew.

Look down on the still village as the morning sun, peering over the hills, sends rays to penetrate the gentle encircling haze. The mill-pond, beginning to gleam in the sun, stands among big trees in a rich meadow sloping towards picturesque cottages. From the cottages rises the smoke of the earliest kindled fires; the smoke curls at first, then rises to a straight blue line slow to disperse in the still air. The village is awakening to the day.

In the distance you can hear the noise of the train so clearly that it is difficult to believe the line is five miles away. The sound lends remoteness to the village, and seems to increase the stillness, which is also enhanced, not broken, by the sudden clamour of cocks and the monotonous plaint of a calf parted from its mother. There is an atmosphere of friendly peacefulness in which unkindness and discontent would seem impossible; even as the sweet air, touched by the savour of the sea on the far side of the Downs, would seem by its sheer sweetness to put all mischievous gossip to shame. Here is the place for a man to live a fruitful, quiet life. No wonder bungalows are springing up on all sides.

Stroll through the village down into the main street to the Square where the motor 'buses stop; round by the Post Office and the vicarage, with its gnarled yew hedge, by the schoolhouse, up to the Monastery – look at the numbers of little houses away on the gorse common – down by the Village Room, where pictures are shown on Friday evenings, past the newly-built Comrades' Hut and into the village square again.

The village is prosperous. There are two general stores and one London emporium, three butchers, four bakers, three cobblers, a barber, three builders; a bank, a dissenting chapel, two cycle shops, three tea shops, a garage, and seven public-houses.

Yes, and in their near neighbourhood there are many residences of wealthy people with town houses, and they take a great interest in the welfare of the village, subscribing to the Flower Show, glad to be vice-presidents of the Village Room and the Cricket and Football Clubs, members even of the Parish Council. Why, one man and his wife are said to have spent eighty thousand pounds in making a large house suitable for their occupation. Fine thing for the village.

Up there? Are they not picturesque, those dear little cottages looking out over the mill-pond? On the doorsteps little children will soon be playing. Yes, one latrine conspicuously outside, for men, women and children – the bucket is emptied once a week. Things are much better than they used to be.

Come away, come away – up this quiet street. Early workmen are starting out now, walking with a long, rolling stride, as though not to disturb the comfortable drowsiness in which their faces are still wrapped. In that yard stands a gay chap whistling loud as he harnesses a white cob; his cheerful, cried-out greetings do not rouse his friends to more than a murmured word and a slow, sagacious nod. 'Take all sorts to make a world!' is a favourite proverb here.

Walk up this quiet street and leave all aching disparities with a prayer for the spread of human kindliness and the growth of human imagination; come away and look at that nice poster hanging in the Post Office window for all who pass to read:

A MATCH

Will be played on SATURDAY,
Against Raveley
Wickets will be pitched at 2.30.

1. Mr. Gauvinier (Capt.)
2. »   Hunter
3. »   Fanshawe
4. »   Bannister
5. »   S. Smith
6. »   Trine

7. Mr. Bannock
8. »   White
9. »   Furze
10. »   Waite
11. »   McLeod

JOHN McLEOD (*Hon. Sec.*)

Scorer: Mr. Allen

Umpire: Mr. Bird

Chapter Two

SOME PLAYERS AWAKEN

On Saturday morning, August 4, 1921, at a quarter past five, Horace Cairie woke up and heard the rustle of wind in the trees outside his bedroom window. Or was it a gentle, steady rain pattering on the leaves? Oh, no, it couldn't be! That would be too rotten. Red sky at night shepherd's delight. And the sky last night had been red as a great rose and redder, simply crimson. 'Now mind, if you over-excite yourself and don't get proper sleep, you won't be able to enjoy the match or anything!' his mother had said, and Horace knew that what she said was true. Still, what was a fellow to do? Turn over and go to sleep? If it rained, it rained, and there was an end of it: his getting up to see whether the pattery, rustly sound was the wind or rain would not alter the weather. For a chap of fifteen and a few months he feared that he was an awful kid.

He got out of bed deliberately as any man and walked to the window. He leaned out as far as he could lean and surveyed the morning sky with the solemnity of an expert.

Not a cloud was to be seen anywhere; only a breath of wind sufficient to rustle a few dried ivy leaves against the window-sill. A delicate haze spread over the country to the hills.

What a day it would be to watch a cricket match, and suppose Joe Furze couldn't turn out and he were asked to play! And suppose, when he went in to bat five runs were wanted and he got a full toss to leg and hit it plumb right for a four and then with a little luck . . . or supposing Tillingfold had batted first and the others wanted six runs and he had a great high catch and held it or a real fast one and jumped out and it stuck in his fingers. Oh, goodness, what a clinking game cricket was! Splendid even to watch. And old Francis always let him mark off the tens and put the figures up on the scoring board.

Meanwhile it was still three good hours to breakfast, and if he curled up in bed and went to sleep the time would pass more quickly, and if he were wanted to play he would be in better form than if he mooched about the garden on an empty stomach.

What a morning! What a morning! What luck!

'Now then, darling, you'll be late for breakfast.'

Horace leaped out of bed at his mother's voice.

'Is old Francis here yet?'

'Been here an hour or more.'

'Has he brought any message?'

'Not that I know of.'

'Oh, curse! Of course I shan't be wanted to play.'

'A very good thing, too, dear. I don't like your playing with men.'

'Oh, rot, mum! What complete piffle! I'm not a kid.'

He kissed her first on one cheek then on the other.

'You will never understand about cricket, will you?'

He began to wash himself with more speed than care, and after a hurried wipe with a towel, climbed into shirt and shorts, slapped his head with two hair brushes while he trod into laceless sand shoes, stooped to tug each over the refractory heel, and fell downstairs, struggling into an ancient blazer.

'Half a sec.!' he shouted in at the open dining-room door and rushed out into the garden to find old Francis. He ran hard towards the potting shed, but seeing Francis sweeping the leaves up on the drive he stopped his swift run, and carefully adjusting his coat collar, strolled up towards him. Old Francis had watched him come tearing out of the house, watched him slow up, knew what he was mad to know: so he went on sweeping with the briefest possible edition of greeting, of which 'orn' was alone audible. After a little he said drily:

'Looks like rain, don't it?'

'Oh, I dunno! No, do you think so?'

'Ah! Uncommon like rain. Smell it everywhere.'

He leaned on his broom and sniffed the air up dubiously. Then he went on sweeping.

'I say!' said the boy. 'Would it be all right if you let me mark off the ones again, do you think? And shove up the numbers.'

'Shouldn't wonder. But there won't be no cricket; not this afternoon.'

'Why not? The rotters haven't scratched, have they?'

'Scratched, not that I knows on. Much sensibler if *we 'ad*, seeing the team as we've had to rake up. Be getting they old chaps from the Union before we're done. Ah! And some on 'em wouldn't be half bad, I lay; not too slippy on their feet.'

He referred thereby to a never-to-be-forgotten occasion (by others, it seemed, at any rate) when Horace in his eagerness to dash in and save one had fallen at full length and the batsman had secured two runs: a blackish day for Horace and a blackish day for his flannels, for the ground was not dry and he had chosen a bare patch on which to lie extended. He let the reference pass with a blush and persisted:

'Why, you don't mean Dick Fanshawe isn't playing?'

'Oh, no, he's all right.'

'Or Teddie White or Sid Smith?'

Old Francis grudgingly asserted that they were certain to turn out.

'Tom Hunter, can't he play?'

'He's game, bless you! Tom not play!'

'Well, who isn't?'

'It ain't so much who isn't as who is!'

He continued sweeping with easy, rhythmical strokes, his dark eyes watching Horace from under thick eyebrows. The rhythmical motion of the broom fascinated the boy, who shifted his feet, thrust his hands into his pockets, began to whistle, half-guessed, yet dared not ask the blunt question which he ached to put.

'You might fetch that barrer down if you like.'

'Well, I said I'd only be half a sec.!'

'Don't then if you don't like.'

Horace ran off for the wheelbarrow, which he set down with a bang, so that the boards for lifting the leaves fell off. 'That's it! Upset the blummin' lot,' said old Francis, flicking stray leaves up on to the near heap.

Slowly stooping with the boards he carefully raised a pile of mould and twigs and leaves, which he deposited and pressed down into the barrow; as he leaned on the boards he said slowly:

'As I was saying, it's who is!'

'What do you mean – who is?'

'Playing! They'll be raisin' a team from the infants next. And Raveley arn't a blind school.'

'Oh, chuck it, Francis, tell us.'

'Tell us! Tell us what? And how about your half sec. or whatever it was, and your porridge getting cold? Never knew such a chap. No, I'm dashed if I did. Still there it is. Mr. Mcleod said to me last night: "Do you think that young Cairie would play to-morrow?" "Play?" I said. "But surely to goodness you don't want . . ." '

'I say, you don't mean it?' asked Horace, tremulous with excitement.

'Yes, I do,' said Francis, changing his manner. 'They were saying how Joe Furze couldn't leave his wife with the moving, and who should they get, and I said why not you; you're mad to play, and arn't too bad in the field, and as likely to make a run or two as any of the rest, so there you are.'

'Oh! I say, you are an old ripper!'

'Bit of a show up, I expect, but never mind!'

'I say, you weren't serious about the rain?'

'Rain!' scoffed old Francis. 'Rain! Why, it couldn't rain, not if it tried ever so. Not to-day. It'll be a fair scorcher and no mistake!'

Horace stretched himself in sheer glee, then made a sudden dive at the ribs of old Francis, on which he landed a friendly punch. Francis raised the broom on high, threatening. 'Now then!' he growled.

The boy collared him round the waist, was undone, raised and used as a weight to press the leaves down in the barrow, tickled meanwhile to helpless laughter.

'I'll learn yer,' declared old Francis. 'And just you slip off to breakfast now, or there'll be trouble. That's right. Scatter them leaves everywhere.'

Six o'clock!

Automatically Mrs. Smith slipped her feet out of bed and twisted up her long hair, sitting on the edge of the bed in which Sid Smith lay asleep by the side of a baby, also sleeping. She kept yawning.

She dressed without hurry or delay, watched by two little boys of three and four, at whom she made, from time to time, expressive gestures suggesting what would happen if they broke the silence. It was clear that another baby was well on the way.

Sid snored and stirred, moving against the baby, who opened his eyes. Mrs. Smith looked at both with annoyance. Not that she was one to stand any nonsense from either.

Fastening her skirt she stepped across the room (a little smaller than young Horace Cairie's room) and leaning her face forward she said in a fierce whisper to the two little boys, who continued their impassive stare:

'You lay there, the two of you, mind.'

And she thrust an inquiring hand under the clothes.

'Tst! Filthy!' she muttered with a look of disgust. 'Wash! Wash! Wash! No end to it!'

In spite of her tousled, unkempt condition, it was still quite possible to recognise the prim parlourmaid of six years before, celebrated for the way she kept her glass, for her fine needlework, and for her immaculate manner and appearance. There was still pride in the poise of her head.

She was no sooner out of the room than Jackie, the eldest boy, leaped out of bed, climbed over the baby, and snuggled up against the sleeping man, who opened his eyes and said gruffly:

'Hullo, matey!' – yawning. Then, ' 'Ere, this ain't Sunday.'

'I say, give us a penny, dad!'

The baby awoke, crying. Sid craned his neck round to inspect him. Then heaved himself round in bed to lift him up. He drew his hand back, scowling.

'Struth, all over the bed-clothes!' Jackie looked unhappy, conscious that he had hit on a wrong morning for a penny.

''Ere!' said his father, 'get out of it!'

Jackie, infant as he was, realised that it would be wiser not to climb across his father, but to make a slight detour by the bottom of the bed. In squeezing out between the end of the bed and the wall, however, he unfortunately dragged down his father's flannel trousers, which were hanging on the rail, a small rent having been stitched up in them on the Friday evening. Making his way on all fours, in a praiseworthy effort to conceal his existence, he, without knowing it, dragged the trousers after him across the room, and just by his own bed, being pleasantly inconspicuous, he sat up, and was seated with damp nightshirt on the trousers, which were not in consequence improved. His little brother, who had watched his progress across the floor, leaning over to see what Jackie was doing, fell out of bed and howled.

'Now then!' shouted Sid, 'you ain't hurt yerself.'

'Just you stop that noise!' came Mrs. Smith's voice from the kitchen beneath.

'The little blighter's pitched himself out of bed!' shouted Sid.

'Ain't hurt, is he?'

'No,' shouted Sid. 'A bit scared!'

'I'll scare him! Young monkey.'

Sid Smith was by no means a brute. But it was an understood thing that, except on Sunday mornings, he did no work of any kind in the house before going to his own work. Fortunately for him, he was able to bear without too much compunction the loud woes of children, unless his head was thick after an exceptionally good time.

Mrs. Smith appeared carrying a tin bowl full of water, which she set on a soap box, a convenient washstand:

'Didn't I tell you not to budge from yer bed?' she said angrily to Jackie, who, not managing to avoid the slap aimed at his ear, howled lustily. Her reaching out for the baby was the sign for Sid to rise, which he did with much yawning and stretching and scratching of his head.

'Stop that blinkin' row,' he announced to the room in general, as he picked a woodbine out of its paper on the mantelpiece, lighted it, and put on his trousers, pants and socks under his long nightshirt.

'A nice mess,' he announced, blowing out a long puff of smoke, and watching his wife undo the baby's napkins.

'Faugh!' said his wife, pitching the dirty napkin on to the floor. 'Wash! Wash! Wash!'

The napkin fell on the trousers, which were now a little way under the small boys' bed. Sid put on his vest and shirt and buckled his belt, and went downstairs in his socks to put on his working boots in the scullery.

The baby was held seated in the bowl crying bravely while Mrs. Smith dexterously wiped it over with a rubber sponge.

'When's this blasted kettle goin' to boil?' came a shout from the kitchen.

'How can I tell?' was the prompt retort.

'Choked up with these great lumps o' coal!'

'Why can't you have set the oil lamp to rights then?' she shouted back, adding softly to herself, 'Great booby! Can't set his hand to nothing!'

'Now then, you two!' she cried to the little boys, as she dried the baby with nimble fingers.

Jackie and his brother climbed out of bed and pulled off their nightshirts, coming very slowly nearer to their mother, who rolled the baby in a blanket and set it, without getting up, on the bed, seizing Jackie's arm on the return swing. Rapidly she topped and tailed each small boy with the same rubber sponge and dried them on a dish-cloth. While she was putting on their shirts, Sid appeared in the doorway, whitening one of his cricket boots, the sight of which always infuriated his wife.

'I'll just put them trousers away,' he said, making towards the bed. 'Where in hell are them trousers?' he cried.

'How should I know where you put 'em? They were mended last night, that's all I know.'

'I laid 'em on the bed-rail, folded.' He was peering behind the bed, under the thrown-back bed-clothes.

'Blinkin' swarm o' kids,' he muttered. 'Home – I don't think. All right for a man, this is.'

'All right, my man. I've got ears in me head.'

'Ah! And look out you don't get a thick ear, my gal, afore you're much older.' He was groping angrily on the floor now – smoke in his eyes from the cigarette end between his lips.

'Blast it!' he cried. 'What's this? Look here.'

And rising slowly he lifted the forlorn, soiled trousers. Dismay extinguished anger on his face. It was only on the cricket field that Sid Smith, a bowler famed for many miles around, was able to feel a man's self-respect.

'I say, Liz, wash 'em through for me, old gal.'

'*H'm!* A likely thing on a Saturday morning too; and you being back for your dinner 'fore I've hardly swept out the bedroom. Cricket! Playing the fine gentleman in your white trousers and your white boots. Fat lot of games a woman gets, don't she?'

'Clean 'em up and run the iron over 'em, Liz,' he pleaded in dejection.

'And who was talkin' of thick ears a moment gone?'

'Go on! You know I don't mean half what I say.'

'Good thing for you you don't. Don't come messin' me about now just because you wants a thing done. Oh, yes, I'll see to 'em.'

'That's a mummy!' cried Sid, hoisting Jackie up, who, thinking the moment

*Automatically Mrs Smith slipped her feet
out of bed and twisted up her long hair.*

favourable, clung round his father's neck whispering hoarsely: 'Give us a penny, dad.' His mind was fixed on a certain brightly-coloured sweet he had seen in Straker's window.

'Not half a sharp kid, is he?' smiled Sid.

'Oh, go on, do, and have your breakfast. You're nothing but a pair of kids the two of you.'

'Want penny too,' began Jackie's small brother, and persisted in his request until both children were let out with a hunk of bread each and strict injunctions on no account to get into mischief or to come bothering back round mum, who was specially busy that morning.

Meanwhile Sid disposed of two large slices of bread and dripping at the corner of the kitchen table, and drank two mugs of tea, after which he set out on the three-mile walk to his work, cad to a bricklayer. He called back to his wife: 'If you're havin' a walk round after tea you might have a look in on the field. We're playin' Raveley, and we could walk home together.'

'Oh, well, I'll see how things go. I may and I mayn't.'

'It's eight o'clock, sir,' said the neat housemaid, as she set the morning tea-tray on the bed-table by the side of Edgar Trine.

'Oh, thanks, Kate, thanks,' said Trine, turning sleepily over.

Kate went noiselessly on the thick carpet, pulling back one heavy curtain after another.

She emptied the water from the basin, wiped it out with a special cloth, set a bright brass can full of boiling water in the shining basin, and wrapped the can in a clean face-towel to keep it warm.

'I say, pour me out a cup of tea, Kate,' came a nice voice from the bed.

'Sugar and milk. Yes, I do hate pouring out tea. I'd almost rather not drink it than pour it out for myself.'

Spoilt young devil! Kate should have thought, no doubt; but she didn't. She liked to pour out young Mr. Edgar's tea. He was always the perfect gentleman.

'Thanks, most awfully. I say, do you mind? In that dinner-jacket pocket, my cigarette case. One left, I'll swear. Thanks. Oh, and matches. Yes; thanks most awfully.'

Kate folded up the dinner-jacket and trousers, to be taken downstairs for brushing; inspected his white shirt, which she considered clean enough to wear for dinner once more; rejected the collar, however, which she put silently into the basket.

'First-rate cup of tea, this, Kate.'

'I'm glad, sir.'

'Pour me out another, there's a dear, good girl.'

She did so.

'You're riding this morning, sir. Miss Emily asked me to remind you.'

'Confound it, so I am. Yes, and playing for the village this afternoon. A heavy day, Kate. What sort of weather is it?'

'Beautiful, sir,' answered Kate, laying out his breeches and underclothing.

'You might ask James to bring the two-seater round about a quarter past two, will you? And I say, do look and see if I've a decent pair of white trousers. Perhaps you wouldn't mind fetching them out of the drawer and letting me have a look.'

Kate brought five pairs and laid them on the bed.

'How all this muck accumulates, I don't know!' he grumbled. 'Not a decent pair among the lot. Such fowl flannel, too, since the war. Pick out the best for me, and see my cricket boots are done, do you mind? And tell that young ass to wipe the white off the edges of the soles and the heels. I say, Kate, is Sid Smith playing to-day?'

'Yes, sir; I expect so.'

'Do you know, if he'd had coaching he'd be a class bowler.'

'He's always been a keen cricketer, sir.'

'Rather. He used to bowl at me, do you remember, when I was a nipper at school? Didn't he marry your sister, Kate?'

'Yes, sir.'

'Got a jolly little family, too, hasn't he?'

'Yes, sir.'

'Lucky beggar!'

Kate hated to cadge, and she could not bring out what was on the tip of her tongue to ask. Her sister had often told her she was a silly to keep herself back; but there! She couldn't ask for things, though it did seem a shame they should by lying where they weren't wanted, and young Mr. Edgar would be only too pleased, if she did ask; he was always so kind and thoughtful.

'Who's the match against – Raveley?'

'Yes, sir, I believe so.' Her chance had gone.

'Best cricket going, village cricket,' said Edgar judicially. 'Real keenness. Oh, I'm all for village cricket. If I were down here more, I wouldn't mind running the show. Breakfast nine, I suppose? All right. Thanks.'

He lounged out of bed as Kate closed the door, into the bathroom, which opened out of his bedroom, and turned on the taps for a tepid bath, into which he poured verbena water.

At three minutes to nine, his toilet complete, he strolled down, fresh and clean, in his riding things to the dining-room, where a large breakfast was brought in at nine

punctually. He topped up with three slices of the best ham, he told the mater, he had tasted for many a long day.

'We may be coming to see the match, dear, this afternoon,' his mother said as she left the dining-room. 'I am so delighted you're playing for the village. With all this discontent that's about nowadays, it is good for them all. I am sure we ought all to mix with the people far more than we do.'

'Go on, Mater,' laughed her son. 'You're becoming a regular Bolshie, we all know that. I only play because I like playing for the village better than playing for the Martlets, say. It may not be such good cricket, but I swear it's a better game.'

Mr. John McLeod, Secretary and Treasurer of the Tillingfold Cricket Club, lifted his round bald head with extreme care not to waken the old lady who lay motionless by his side, and turned it slowly in her direction. Through the curtains filtered dim light, by which he saw that her eyes were closed; but as he began to screw his legs out of bed the eyes opened, twinkling.

He lay back laughing. 'Done again, by the Lord, done again! Oh, you, Maria!'

She laughed, too, a pleasant chuckle.

'Don't I know you're like a boy with his stocking on a Christmas morning any day of a cricket match? Just you lay still now, please.'

There they lay – round, stoutish, smiling, rubicund; two tumps, two ducks.

'Ah! I must give up cricket Maria.'

'Nonsense, John. And you enjoying it so!'

'Ah, yes! Maria, before it gives up me. Give the young 'uns a chance, too. I'm slow between the wickets now, Maria.'

'Don't talk so silly, John, please.'

'Bless the woman, if she's not lighted the spirit-lamp and the kettle's on the boil, and me thinkin' I'd surprise her with a nice hot cup of tea as soon as her blessed eyes opened.'

'Got took in this time, didn't you, John?' said Maria, quietly wetting the tea in the pot.

'Not the first time either, by the Lord! Not the first time either!' he cried, enjoying the joke hugely. Maria was pulling up the blind. 'I knew it! A perfect day.' His thoughts ran on. 'And the trouble there is sometimes to get a team together. By the Lord, you'd think you was wantin' 'em to go to the dentist. It's that war's upset us all. And no wonder. Grumble, grumble, grouse, grouse! If it's not one thing, it's another. What a delicious cup of tea, Maria! Dee-licious! Ah! things won't never be the same again. Still, what's it matter? We have glorious, nice games, and if they must grouse, let 'em. Dee-licious cup o' tea, Maria. I'll have another!'

It was poured out for him.

'My goodness! If only Mr. Gauvinier had a little tact! He's a good captain, a first-rate captain. He knows the game in his bones and nothing's too much trouble. But he's 'asty. He can't help himself, he's 'asty. *"Always try a catch, Mr. Skinney!"* he sings out.' The memory tickled him. He repeated the words with a singular relish: ' *"Always try a catch, Mr. Skinney!"* Well, Walter Skinney thought it wiser to take a step back. Don't blame him, the ball was travelling, and him nicely in the deep, a stinger, cruel; and Wally he swears it wasn't no catch, and won't be shouted at before everybody, not he, at his time of life, as though he were a bloomin' nipper who didn't know the difference between a long hop and a catch. And of course, catch or no catch, there wasn't no *use* in shoutin'. And there's plenty say he's conceited. Well, he may be. Anyhow, he knows his own mind, and the deuce of it is he's so often right. But out it always comes; plump and square. No tact, I say, no tact. Still, there it is. I like the beggar. Lord, Maria, I'd do anything for that fellar!'

'The club wouldn't be much without you, John. That's all I know.

'Oh, I help, yes, I help. Bless my soul! I've always had the luck, Maria. Here we are. Nice little house in a beautiful village. Comfortable; son doing well; daughter married. Just the job I love, arranging the matches, smoothing things down, name on card; oh, capital; gives you a little niche in the life of the place. And at the bottom they're as good-hearted a lot of chaps as you could find. All of them; or nearly all of them. And they haven't all of 'em had our luck, Maria.'

'You've deserved your luck, John,' said his wife, earnestly.

At that he became very grave.

'You can't say that, Maria. You can't say that, my dear. There's a many I've met in life as have deserved far more than I have, and met nothing but trouble, trouble, trouble; one trouble after another. Terrible. And they've stuck it and carried on, when I'd 'ave been smashed up and broken, Maria; stuck it too and carried on without a one like you always there to help. Oh! there are good men in this world; good, brave men.'

'Yes, and some mean, bad ones, too, John.'

'Ah! well, that's true; and I sometimes wonder there ain't more. That's a fact, I do. But bless my soul, Maria, I wish they'd get together a bit more. We could make that ground the prettiest little ground in England. It's getting better, of course. But what can you do, when the football starts in September, playing over the square; when any turf needs a good dressing and a rest? It is fair heart-breaking!'

'Oo-ah! That's a nasty twinge. I'll have to get you to give me back a rub, Maria, my dear. This'll have to be my last season, I fear. Give the young 'uns a chance! Of course I'm all right at point – no running to do, and if a smartish one comes I can get to it pretty quick, and I don't say it's not as likely to stick in my hand as not: but a sudden stoop! That's where the bother of it is; a sudden stoop! Well, I can't, and I'm not as fast as I was between the wickets, Maria, though being a judge of a run and backing up properly I'm not so slow as some. But that sudden stoop, Maria. Ah, well, can't be done, and there's an end of it, can't – be – done! Just look at it! What a perfect day! Just look at it, now, I ask you.'

'Yes, but a nasty cold breeze comes creeping up so often; and I do hope you'll be sensible and wear your nice, warm undervest, John. It holds closer to the skin; and if you wear a nice bow tie on your cricket shirt, the collar'll not flap open and no one won't see as you're wearing a undervest.'

'I'm not vain, Maria, as you know, my dear. But I do hate to appear ridic'lous; and I heard one of the toffs say of someone else: "My God! Look, he's wearin' an underfug." That was the word he used. "Underfug." There's etiquette, you know, Maria, and there's a deal more than comfort to be thought of in clothes.'

'I never heard such nonsense, John. Toff or no toff, I think it a most vulgar expression.'

'One's very sensitive about these little things, Maria. I don't know why one should be. Always at the beginning, you know, when one walks on to the field first; you don't know how shy I always feel. I believe other fellows do, too, somehow; but one can't mention it. Of course it passes off as soon as the game begins. I don't believe wild horses, now, could drag me on to the field in one of them little blazer things, *you know* – it would seem so unsuitable.'

'Well, I never, John, and men talk of women being vain.'

'Ah, it's not quite vain. It's sensitive, Maria; sensitive to the eyes of others.'

Meanwhile, Mrs. McLeod was dressed, and helping John into an old woolly jacket.

She set a large board on his knee and a book; for John had been a sign-writer, and his hobby other than secretarial duties of the Tillingford Cricket Club was the making of manuscript books. Many who were not interested in cricket would stop to admire the calligraphy of the club notices, the list of teams, and so forth, exhibited in the Post Office window.

'The height of luxury! Did anyone see the like of this, now?' John McLeod commented as these arrangements were being made. 'Waited on like a lord. Breakfast in bed! Well, I never. No man ever had such a wife!'

'Ah!' she laughed. 'I know you well enough by this time, my boy. If I didn't keep you safe in bed, you'd be running round all over the place wearin' yourself out, and by the time the day was done, what with you and your cricket, I should be having a sick man on my hands.'

She left him happily at work, the two pillows behind his back, the bolster on end, the board of his own making leaning on his doubled-up knees. He hummed while he worked – tunes of a melancholy grandeur, which was in odd contrast with the rubicund, cheery face; a blended tune which for the most part opened with 'Sun of my Soul, thou Saviour dear,' and somehow got lost in the heaving sorrow of 'the long, long way to go.' Perhaps the melancholy drone was useful in damping his good spirits down to the accurate precision required in the performance of his work. It was years since he had made a blot.

Breakfast was at length brought in. Coffee, toast (in rounds), two boiled eggs, some hot rashers of bacon: the board was removed, a large napkin tied round his neck, in case of any little accidents, dear, as she said, and he had nothing to do but tuck in, as he said.

'Oh, Maria, Maria! You spoil me, my dear. No wonder I've got a girth when you bring up such a breakfast, knowing well as I can never resist a good breakfast, never. But would you say now, as how, generally speaking, I did eat particular 'earty? Yet here I am, round as a barrel, and getting rounder, whereas old Silas Ragg, he's thin as a lath, and tough as wire, and he won't never see six-and-fifty again, and can bowl all afternoon easy as an old machine and never turn a hair. It 'ud kill me to bowl three overs.'

'You must have plenty of nourishing food in you, fat or no fat, when you're going to take all that exercise. Wringing wet with perspiration you gets: and your system must be kep' up somehow. But this little parcel come from the stores.'

She produced a large envelope stuffed with something soft, which John pinched thoughtfully: 'No, it can't be them!' he ruminated.

'Never knew Mr. Boyle before his word. "This week ain't possible, Mr. McLeod," he said, "not if I stretches a point ever so." By the Lord, it is them, though!' he cried, eagerly pulling out a dozen sky-blue cricket caps.

'Now, please,' said his wife, 'finish your breakfast while the coffee's hot.'

'Here we are, seven and three-quarters,' said John, after some fumbling among the

*'Oh, Maria, Maria! You spoil me . . . It'd kill me to bowl
three overs.'*

caps, too engrossed to hear any plea for delay. 'Just hold that mirror up, my love,' he went on, fitting the cap on his bald head. 'How's that now? Something like, eh? How's it suit me? A bit more over the forehead, don't you think? So. They're cunning little chaps and no mistake; work out at three bob a-piece too with the monogram.'

'Fine!' said Mrs. McLeod. 'I'm sure it's a mere boy you look in that little hat. But you must finish your breakfast now, or I shall get vexed with you.'

She had been trying her best not to laugh; the sight of her husband's gleeful old countenance under the little cricket cap as he sat up in bed proved too much for her, and she shook with laughter as she leaned forward to pat his face so that his feelings, always a little touchy on the score of appearance, might not be hurt.

John laughed, too, but not quite so whole-heartedly.

'You was always one to laugh,' he said. 'Bless you! But, Maria, my dear, I don't look ridic'lous now, do I?' he added, on such a note of anxiety that she forced control for a moment to answer:

'Ridic'lous – not you!'

But his earnest look promptly overcame her.

'Perhaps I had better keep to my old cloth cap,' he spoke regretfully. 'I'm used to it. And so are the others.'

She moved her hands in strenuous denial and shook her head from side to side. At length she managed to say:

'Oh, I'm not laughing *at* you, like: no indeed; I wouldn't do such a thing, but, oh! you are such an old dear.'

'Magnificent idea! These little caps, you know.' Mrs. McLeod was carefully wiping her eyes with her pocket handkerchief, relapsing into good-humoured laughter from time to time. 'Ted Bannister's idea. Makes all the difference to the look of a team.'

'Oh, dear!' crooned Mrs. McLeod. 'Will Mr. Bannister be wearing one too, then?'

'Of course he will, my dear,' said John, becoming a little severe.

'What time will the match begin?'

'The usual time. Wickets pitched at 2.30,' he quoted the official list which hung in the Post Office window, as though to assert his dignity. But he could not withstand the infection of his wife's merriment as she faltered: 'Oh! I'll be there – with Mrs. Bannister.'

So John began to chuckle:

'Ah! There won't half be some leg-pulling, I lay a sovereign. You should have heard 'em on at each other at the meeting. Old Teddie White, he swore as he'd never wear one. Obstinate devil, and I don't believe he will. Won't make himself a figure of fun. Old-fashioned, that's what they are. Sticks to their 'abits like their skins, and a sight closer some on 'em. Old Henry, he's always sore about the gentry havin' more chances and all that humbug. If we all wears 'em, Lord bless my soul, it'll fair put the wind up those Raveley chaps. We'll have 'em beat before the coin's tossed.'

'Oh, dear!' said Maria, feebly, 'it'll be good as a play to see you all.'

'Yes,' said John, meditatively. 'I think I'll just stroll round and give 'em out this morning like. More chance to get the chaps to wear 'em p'raps.'

'Oh, no, you don't!' said Maria, with an amazing access of resolution. 'Not you, my boy! You don't stir from that bed now, please, till eleven o'clock. They may want warning' (here laughter took her) 'to be prepared, but you really mustn't move, John, and get tiring yourself out.'

He was turning the cap on his fist, studying the cut and the monogram.

'Try it once more, dear,' she begged.

He obeyed. She was enchanted.

'I mustn't forget to pull him well down over the forehead,' he said with great gravity.

'No,' she agreed. 'Not on any account.'

'You won't get laughing too much on the cricket field now, will you?' he said, rather shyly.

'Oh, no!' she answered very demurely. 'I hope I know by this time what's proper.'

She removed the breakfast things and left him with his board upon his knees. But no tune of even the most melancholy grandeur could keep his thoughts from wandering on towards all the incomprehensibly unnecessary unhappiness which he knew existed in the beautiful village: the crossness, the unkindness, the gossip. 'Ah, they've not all had your luck, my boy,' he said to himself to appease his anger. 'Suppose you had to shovel rubble all day like Sid Smith, where'd your temper be of an evening; or to do any work you couldn't fancy, with another chap bossing you all the time. Who's really happy now in this village? Oh dear! Oh dear! Oh dear! If it's not one thing, it's another!'

He leaned back gazing forlornly at his board, to which he suddenly gave a severe blow.

'Driftin' into the miserables,' he said to himself. 'Driftin' into the miserables! What use is there in that now – on a perfect morning, with a glorious game of cricket waiting for me this afternoon. By the Lord Harry! It's best not to think of some things.'

'Maria!' he called very loud. 'Maria!'

She was on the landing and opened the door almost immediately.

'Yes, John, what's the matter?'

'Ah, well, now you mustn't be cross, my dear; but I can't lie on here. Really I can't. What with the match and the caps coming and all, I'm too excited. I can't keep quiet and do me writing. My thoughts go rushing about all over the place to where they've no business at all, no business at all.'

'You're a wilful man, John,' she said, smiling. 'Most wilful. But you must promise me to wear your undervest, now, won't you?'

'All right, my dear,' he agreed a little ruefully. 'I promise, if it'll make your mind easier.'

'Oh, far easier, John, far easier,' she answered him.

Chapter Three

THE MORNING PASSES

Tom Hunter had hardly entered his shop, and was still helping the breadcrust out of his teeth, which the doctor had told him the evening before should all be extracted, with his tongue and a split match, when he saw young Joe Mannerly come down the street, pushing along a bicycle which belonged he knew for certain, to Paul Gauvinier.

'Mornin', Tom,' said young Joe cheerfully. 'The Boss wants you to mend a puncture in the back wheel, and while you're about it, he says, you might give the old bike a good oilin' all over.'

'All right!' said Tom, thoughtfully sucking the match, and proceeding to insert the point with some difficulty in the far corner of his mouth. Young Joe looked on attentively.

'Busy this morning, then?'

Tom Hunter paid no heed to the insinuation.

'Thought you was done with cricket.'
'Damn soon shall be,' Tom Hunter growled.

'Bike spokes come in wonderful handy for that job,' the boy went on.

Tom Hunter turned serious eyes upon him, disdaining from ten years' superiority in age any precocious effort at humour. Everyone knew that Joe Mannerly was a cheeky young devil, every bit the same as his father before him, elders would add. A good enough kid, of course, for all that, and a favourite with Tom Hunter, when he was in a good temper which was less seldom the case than it used to be before he was affected by trench fever and poison gas.

'Boss says he'll fetch it later on.'

'Good for 'im,' grunted Tom, chewing the match.

'Got to lose 'em, I hear,' Joe threw out by way of conversation, for he liked to talk and be seen talking with Tom Hunter, who was Tillingfold's best forward and one of the hardest hitters in the cricket eleven – especially to be seen talking thus man to man by a group of little school-boys and girls, mere children, dawdling on their way to the swings on the Recreation Ground.

'Lose 'em! Lose what?' Tom growled, so surlily that Joe's self-possession flickered.

'Y'r teeth,' he said as airily as possible, feeling the eyes of the whole group staring at him.

'What a place!' sneered Tom Hunter, 'what a cacklin' bloody 'ole of gossip! Only knew of it myself last night.'

'Mrs. Hawkins mentioned it to mother. That's all. They was sorry.'

'And who the 'ell mentioned it to Mrs. 'Awkins?' P'raps she could tell yer mother what I 'ad for breakfast this morning.'

'Make a pretty fairish guess, I lay a tanner.'

Tom Hunter spat the match out contemptuously.

'Got the rats, then, Tom?' (Tom ignored the kind inquiry.)

'Here, lean the bike up against that wall.'

Young Joe ventured to carry on the conversation.

'Not playin' this afternoon, I suppose?'

'Ain't you seen the list, then?'

'Thought you was done with cricket, after last Saturday.'

'Damn soon shall be,' he growled, turning the bicycle upside down so that it rested on the seat and handle-bars. 'It's a disgrace the way things is done now. Selection Committee. Faugh! It's just a click, that's all that is. Ah!' he threatened with terrible significance, 'I shan't keep my mouth shut much longer. I'll have some things to say to one or two of 'em before any of us is much older. Same old lot always playin'! Sickenin'! Look here! If a bloke joins a club he wants a game, don't he? Well, what I say is, he ought to get it: and a different chap ought to get up the team each week; all friendly and comfortable like it used to be and give every member his chance of a game. Gentlemen's Cricket Club, that's what I calls it.'

He was savagely working the tyre loose: all the more savagely because he felt it unsportsmanlike to be talking in this way to young Joe, who was a mere nipper, and whom he half suspected of laughing at him. In his heart Tom Hunter was a thorough sportsman and hated the inclination to grouse which he knew was growing on him but which he did not unfortunately know how to overcome. Young Joe twinkling said:

'What I says is: everyone should crowd on and play; the whole lot of 'em. The more the merrier! Gals too. The whole blinkin' crowd. Have some fun then. Cooh! Lumme! Some one 'ud have to go in last for all that!'

'Go on, yer silly young fool!' said Tom Hunter sternly. 'About time you got back to your work 'stead of loafin' round here, talkin' so stoopid!'

'Mind you lift one or two into the pond, Tom!' said Joe, laughing.

'I'll lift someone else into the pond, my man, if you don't look slippy,' said Tom, taking an angry step towards the boy, who ran; to turn at a safe distance with a loud cry of 'Good-bye-ee,' after which he went off whistling and pleased to think he had 'pulled old Tom's leg.' He stopped whistling to greet a very solid man almost as thick as he was long who was carrying, with great care, an extremely small basket with three eggs in it.

'Mornin', Mr. Bird!' sang out young Joe.

Sam Bird answered: 'Good-mornin', Joe!' with an air of surprise, as though the boy had been invisible until he spoke, and continued his difficult advance. Sam Bird, with or without a small basket with eggs in it, habitually walked with diffidence, as though at each step his feet apologised for placing so much weight upon the earth's surface. He walked habitually as men walk in a sick-room to prevent their boots from creaking, and his gait was in fantastic contrast to the bulk of his person. He spoke, too, with a kind of frail brightness, though one might have expected a stentorian note to issue from so stout a trumpet as his thick neck and wide-mouthed face suggested. He had played cricket for Tillingfold before Tom Hunter's parents had begun to walk out together, and he knew the name and deeds of every man who had played first-class cricket within the last forty years and more. His opinion on any of the many subtle points that arise in the game of cricket was valuable; of the club itself he was a thick, sound prop. In his careful progress up the street he edged towards the cycle shop. Tom Hunter looked up and said less glumly than he had spoken to young Joe:

'H'lo, Sam!'

'H'lo, Tom!' answered Bird, and stopped.

'A lovely morning!' he went on after a moment's pause, a smile widening over his immense face. 'In my opinion, it's likely to be hot this afternoon. A real hot scorcher.' He put his head a little on one side. 'Just your day, too. You always take a few off Raveley, I've noticed.'

'Oh, might, you know. Might. If I don't get too straight a one in the first over.'

Sam laughed. 'Ah! These first overs. They've been the undoing of a goodish few. Wonderful what a lot of ways there are of gettin' out when you first stand up; and after you've been there for a bit, blessed if it's not a surprise you ever could get out! Very glad you're able to play, though.'

'Why shouldn't I be able to play, then?' He was instantly on the defensive, remembering Sam's presence in the Village Room during his outburst that he was done with cricket.

'Well, I heard say as you'd trouble with your teeth.'

'Lord! If that ain't the bloomin' limit. Whoever heard of such a place? Doctor says last night – I'd been to get some med'cine – "Let's look at your mouth, Tom. Yes, you'd be better without that lot. They're rotten." You know his straight way?'

Sam Bird assented with a sagacious shake of his heavy head, a convincing, expressive shake.

'I didn't tell even me sister; and here this morning young Joe Mannerly – cheeky young devil – '

'He is that,' Sam interrupted to agree.

' "Losin' y'r teeth, then," he says. Whole blasted village knows it. How's it done? That's what beats me.'

'Every time. Mar-villous! Mrs. Harris mentioned the fact to me.' He spoke in a propitiatory tone.

'Same with everything. Gossip, gossip, gossip! Nothin' but back-chat. If a feller's got a grievance, why the 'ell can't he spit it out at a meetin' that's for the purpose? With the cricket it's fair sickenin'. Don't they do their best? Grant you, they make mistakes. Who wouldn't? I wouldn't stand it if I was them. What d'ye hear all over the place, in every corner? "Nice thing. Same old lot playin' again. What we wants is a Working Men's Club." No, Goveneer's about right. There are sportsmen and others. He says it sarky-like and sneering, but it's the bleedin' truth. And most of 'em's others!'

'When you've lived as long as me, Tom, you'll find you'll get used to grousin'. Why, I've heard you do a bit of that y'rself. I know I've groused a bit in my time: that's a fact I have. But we have spankin' fine games. So what does it matter?'

'Ah!' said Tom, curiously unconvinced. 'But it ain't right, Sam. All this back-chat gets up my sleeve. Choppin' and changin'. Sayin' one thing to a man's face and another behind his back. Ah! I shall have somethin' to say to some on 'em before we're any of us much older! I won't mention no names, but I know what I know, and there's one or two will 'ave to be mentioned.'

There was a pause after this dark threat, a hush perceptible. For Sam Bird knew well, and Tom Hunter was aware that he knew well, who was one of the guiltiest of the grousers: and this knowledge lent a touch of awkwardness to the situation.

'Well,' said Sam at length judicially, 'as I've often remarked it's an imperfect world, Tom, an imperfect world.'

At which they wished each other 'so long' and Sam pursued his careful course up the street, smiling ever the more broadly as he left Tom Hunter further behind.

'I'll be jiggered!' he said to himself in slow and massive glee, 'if that don't beat cock-fightin'! Whoever started the talk of the Gentlemen's Cricket Club if he warn't

Tom Hunter! Bless'd if a man can believe his own ears!'

And he thoughtfully rubbed his own ear, which was large-lobed and very hairy.

Meanwhile Tom Hunter, looking up as Sam's broad back disappeared from sight, said to himself: 'All right, gettin' half a crown for standin' umpire with y'r tea thrown in. Always number one comes first. *Ev'ry* – time.'

As a matter of fact, Sam Bird invariably paid for his tea; but it is natural for a young man who has been informed on the previous evening that his teeth should be extracted, to take a not too kindly or accurate view of this imperfect world, as Sam Bird most wisely called it.

Soon after breakfast, while Paul Gauvinier was working (he was an artist) a message came that Bill Bannock, who kept wicket for Tillingfold, was unable to play. Furious, he went to find the messenger and discover, if possible, the reason of Bill's non-appearance: the messenger, a red-faced boy on a bicycle, couldn't rightly say for certain, but he rather thought that his people were coming down (meaning Bannock's employer). Gauvinier swiftly recognised the futility of anger at the messenger, not, however, before it had been exhibited; and being grimly aware of his own folly at the exhibition, he was not enlivened in spirit. 'Thanks!' he said to the boy. 'We'll easily find someone to take his place. You might thank him for letting me know in such good time.'

The boy grinned and mounted his bicycle. In a moment or two Gauvinier called out to him to stop, thinking that perhaps a taint of unnecessary sarcasm lurked in the message, and as he prided himself on his great tact, he thought it wiser to leave the message unsent. But as he walked up to the boy it occurred to him that anyhow the message would be delivered, so he contented himself with saying:

'We should have been let down badly if Mr. Bannock hadn't taken the trouble to send you along. I've known fellows just not turn up and say nothing.'

And he presented the boy with threepence. The boy rode off chuckling to think that old Gauvinier hadn't half got his rag out about Bill.

Of course, thought Gauvinier, it would have happened just the morning on which he had sent his bicycle to be mended. Bill Bannock was the Trines' head gardener, and as the Trines came down from town every week-end through the summer and Bannock went round the grounds with Mr. Trine on the Sunday morning, there was probably some other reason for his abstention from the game. Gauvinier had not far to seek for that other reason. He remembered his suggestion, made on the previous Saturday, that Bannock should stand a foot further behind the wicket than was his custom so that he should not, as he not infrequently did, knock down the wicket with his left foot. One batsman had appealed in consequence of this against the fact that he had been bowled and retired grumbling. 'Does he or doesn't he?' Gauvinier had asked himself a hundred times, and in spite of his horror at such a proceeding, he was unwillingly coming to the opinion that he sometimes did – not intentionally, but taking swift advantage of an accident. So a certain relief at Bannock's inability to play was mingled with his annoyance at having to find a substitute. He would have to ask Jim Saddler, as a personal favour, to play: as a personal favour because, though Jim was eager to play, he felt that it was due to his dignity as a man to resent being asked to play at the last moment; a stop-gap not posted on the list. His wife, moreover, kept him well up to the mark in this attitude, lynx-eyed for an affront to the family prestige.

'Nothing else to do but run round after these ill-behaved babies! Suppose I'd had a sitter!' Gauvinier thought, for the personal dignity taint is more swiftly infectious than measles. From that he took off to the idea that his effort to spread goodwill by good cricket had only stirred a hornet's nest of touchiness and malice. After all, cricket was an absurdity. A man grown to man's estate should put away childish things. But from this staid truth he shook himself with a laugh and called out to young Joe, who was tidying the paths.

Young Joe had seen the messenger arrive, and had quickly put two and two together, having heard the report of Mr. Bannock's anger at the suggestion that he should stand a foot further behind the wicket. All his young enthusiasm plumped for the Boss. He had spoken out on one occasion in the Reading Room and his mind had been thrown into an incoherent turmoil by Mr. Skinney remarking: 'Good for you, young Joe: you know which side y'r bread's buttered.'

'Just run down into the village,' Gauvinier said, 'there's a good chap, and fetch up my bike. I've got to find a substitute for Mr. Bannock, who can't play this afternoon.'

'Yes, sir!' Joe answered, making off for his jacket; but he had not put his arms into the sleeves before he was called back.

'All right, Joe, it'll be quicker if I fetch it myself.'

The boy, disappointed in his chance of helping, objected: 'I could get down in six minutes: ride back in three or four; you've got to shave.'

Paul loved every sign of the boy's attachment.

'Well, perhaps it would be more convenient if you don't mind.'

Whereupon Joe set off at an earnest trot, regardless of the morning's heat; and Paul, restored by this eager willingness to complete good humour, went into the house to shave.

Saddler's keenness for a game of cricket under any conditions was so great that the subtlest ingenuity would be required to make it clear that Gauvinier realised he only consented to play at considerable inconvenience and with extreme reluctance, solely as a personal favour to the Captain. Young Joe's allegiance enabled Paul to relish the fun of the situation: without it he would probably have sunk too deep into the sad marsh of human unhappiness, into which, being of an affectionate nature, he was all too apt to sink, especially during this summer, when a friend's defection had inclined him to think it an everlasting impossibility that human beings should ever live simply and love each other, as they all, without knowing it, longed to do.

By the time he was ready Joe had returned with a shining, sweaty face, declaring that he had taken eight and a half minutes and that the half-minute was due to Tom Hunter's slackness in not letting him shift the bicycle which leaned against the Boss's.

'It's ninepence,' Joe announced, and added angrily under his breath: 'And I can mend punctures.' With 'stupid fool not to let me!' plainly understood. Some are nicer than you dare to hope, and some are worse than you like to think, was Gauvinier's sententious comment to himself as he said: 'You're a damn good chap, young Joe!' and rode off on his bicycle.

He was right in surmising that he would be in time to catch Saddler in the kitchen garden and, after making a discreet entry up the back drive, found him lifting lettuces with the help of an elderly under-gardener.

At sight of him the colour deepened on Saddler's face with a rush of boyish hope, obvious in spite of his grizzled face and austere, if not heavy, bearing. His eyes brightened. Courteously, being on his own ground, he came a few steps forward to greet Gauvinier, who after a little, came to the point:

'Same old story, Jim. We're in a hole and you've got to help us out. Jolly good thing we've got just a few people who think more of the club than of themselves. You couldn't possibly play this afternoon, I suppose?'

'This afternoon!' repeated Sadler, as though he were completely taken aback by the suggestion.

'Yes; this afternoon.'

'I suppose old Bill Bannock's let you down.'

Little lifts to his head showed all-knowing criticism.

'His governor's got to see him unexpectedly.'

Their eyes met. Jim scratched his head, breathing a husky laugh.

'We know all about that,' he said. 'But I'm with you all along; there's no sense in standing up so bloody near the wickets. It's nothing else but foolishness. We're playing Raveley, is it?'

'Yes.'

'Well!' said Saddler, with a sort of mysterious glee. 'It just so happens as I can't play, not this afternoon. I more than half promised the missus to run down into Seapoint for some shopping.'

'What a pity!' said Paul. 'Of course you couldn't possibly put that off! I shouldn't dream of asking you to put that off.'

Jim Saddler looked straight at him; then began to chuckle.

'No! I know you wouldn't. Oh, no! Not you! I think you'd ask a bloke to put his bloody marriage off for a game of cricket. You arn't half a deep one. Sayin' that soft, too – I shouldn't dream of . . . No, I lay you wouldn't.'

Gauvinier shared his mirth, and they both laughed more freely than boys.

'That's capital! You'll play, then. I always love having you on the side.' Which was quite true, as Saddler made up in keenness what he lacked in skill. Jim became very serious, however, to remark:

'Mind you this! I don't hold with such goings-on! I'm glad to oblige you, but there's some on 'em I'd see farther first.' He shook his head ominously and spat: 'Ah, a deal farther!'

At first Gauvinier had endeavoured to probe these frequent dark threats and hinted mysteries, but he had for some time desisted from the attempt; and now he contented himself with trying to emulate, without much success, the tremendous sagacity of a silent head-shake. He feared that his head was not quite large and solid enough for the purpose; and he regretted this deficiency as a dog might who had never learned to express emotion by the carriage of his tail.

'Well, Colonel Mowly, what's your opinion of the country, eh? Going to the dogs. Yes, yes, going to the dogs, I thought so.'

Dick Fanshawe rubbed with one finger the cheek of the large tubby cat, sitting on the newspaper, which lay on the breakfast table, and the cat rose slowly with tail erect and arched back to push a chubby, furry cheek against the extended palm. The friendly fellow began a sonorous purr of much dignity, treading his claws out thoughtfully on the crackly paper. The fat cheeks were gently rubbed with both Dick Fanshawe's to Colonel Mowly's great contentment.

In bounced upon this ruminant scene a small boy of seven, who pushed the startled cat leaping from the table and jumped upon his father's knee, declaring in tones indicative of an outraged moral sense:

'How could you, dads? You know Pussums mustn't be on the table. And here you are sitting on here and on and on and you've got your boots to whiten and your bat to oil and Mrs. Preust is waiting to clear away, and you said you wouldn't have a practice knock with me in the garden 'cos you had so much work to do this morning. It's not fair, not a bit fair!'

And he thumped his father angrily upon the chest. Colonel Mowly stood staring out of the window flicking his tail from side to side in anger at this Bolshevik treatment of his highness, and then departed without loss of dignity to find a favourite hot spot under a wall on which to sleep out the morning, and very likely the afternoon too, if all went well.

Dick Fanshawe bore up against this whirlwind of reproach: and regarded the small lump of exuberance with smiling, solemn eyes.

'It's not fair,' the monster persisted, scowling. 'It's not fair. You ought either to *do* your work or have a game with me or something. Instead of which you just sit here and talk to that beastly cat, who can't understand a word you say. And I've got nothing to do.'

'I'm sorry, but it's no good trying to bully me, old man. I'm going to work and write letters till twelve; then you can help me whiten my boots and oil my bat and put me down one or two straight ones in the garden.'

Dick got up so that Oliver was deposited on his feet, still angry, but trying to climb through his angriness.

'Who's Henry Waite, anyhow?' he asked in a cross voice.

'He's a dark horse,' answered his father.

'What do you mean, dark horse?'

'No one knows how he plays.'

'What's he playing for then?'

'He may be very good.'

'I 'spect he's very bad. Jack Skinney thinks his dad ought to be playing.' Oliver cheered up at the memory; and added with intense conviction: 'He's rotten. I say, must you really work and write beastly letters? 'Cos if you must I shall make a prison cell of mecanno and pretend you're locked and barred and mouldering inside like the bloke in the pictures.'

'I hate the word bloke, old man.'

'I don't. I think it's a jolly good word.'

'Mum and I hate it.'

'It's no use arguing about that, anyhow. You've often told me tastes differ.'

As Dick wandered off into his study, his thoughts ran back to his own boyhood, where rigorous obedience to authority was exacted; and he wondered for a moment whether he would prefer an obedient son to this tempestuous, naked monster who was his friend; a terrible, fierce, exacting friend, for the most part, with sudden lapses into unutterable dearness. Of course there was no choice really; but for all that, the strain of living in the searching light of a live small boy's remorseless vigour was not easy, unless one could live in one's own way with equal vigour.

And from this it may be gathered that Mr. Richard Fanshawe was a man in a million, having an innate sense of reverence for the personality of another, even when that other was his own son.

He was trying to translate a poem of Verlaine, fascinated by the poet's directness of speech, the child's terrible simplicity.

J'ai la fureur d'aimer. Mon cœur si faible est fou.

He brooded intensely over the poem, warm in the sunshine of the language, sensitive to the poem's strange sadness, its trembling loneliness, its vivid sympathy with sorrow.

J'ai la fureur d'aimer. Q'y faire? Ah, laissez faire!

Between the first line and the last, with its haunting repetition, the lifetime of a heart's experience seemed delicately sung; the voice of how many hearts that are dumb!

He heard steps on the drive and looked up to see Gauvinier wheeling his bicycle down the drive. Between the two men there was friendship, that gift of the kind gods, which is so poorly enjoyed.

Clamorous shouting was heard, for Oliver, as he wrought the iron cage for his miscreant father, had spied the newcomer and had dashed out full of righteous indignation, to ward off the interloper. Richard was in time to hear his offspring assert defiantly: 'You can't see dad, Polly. He's got to work and write letters till twelve, and then we're going to whiten his boots and have a knock in the garden and oil his bat.'

Richard's head looked out of the study window and, to Oliver's furious dismay, he said: 'Come in, Polly.'

'No: go away, Polly,' the monster wailed. 'You're not wanted. You'll upset our whole morning.'

'Now then, young Oliver Cromwell, that's a nice cheery welcome,' said Gauvinier, leaning his bicycle against the wall.

'I'm Oliver Fanshawe: not Oliver Cromwell, and I tell you dad's busy.'

'Look here, old man,' said Dick from the window, 'visitors are different from people you live in the same house with always.'

'There's always something!' said Oliver crossly and added: 'What's Henry Waite like, anyhow?' As though, now Gauvinier had come he might, at any rate, be of some use.

'He's pretty good, I believe.'

'Well, you're wrong. He's rotten. Dad says he's a dark house.'

Both men laughed. Dick said, 'Horse, you mean,' and asked Paul to come into the study. To Oliver the world seemed black with deceit and treachery, as he inherited his father's intensity of purpose. But defiance oozed rapidly out and he looked listless and miserable. Gauvinier stooped down to whisper: 'P'raps we'll trick him out for a knock sooner than twelve.'

Oliver instantly chuckled, but he said: 'No fear: you'll go on talking over that rotten French stuff.' And he mooched off, disconsolate, to pour his woes out to his mother.

Paul was admitted into the study, and into the mood of brooding intensity within its owner's heart; for almost anything either deeply felt could be shared (mutely or otherwise) with the other, owing to the kind gods' gift of friendship.

'Look at this,' said Dick, pointing with a pencil to the lines:-

> Mais sans plus mourir dans son ennui
> Il embarque aussitôt pour l'île des Chimères
> Et n'en apporte rien que des larmes amères
> Qu'il savoure, et d'affreux désespoirs d'un instant.

'The clear voice of aching loneliness! Of the whole world's longing for love.'

Paul was engrossed in the lines.

'Awful!' he muttered. 'He leaves no rag of covering. Leaves me naked and full of fear and weak and hopeless. As though all courage must be an imposture. It's all so hideously clear and articulate. *Qu'il savoure!* Ah, the devil!'

He looked up with fear into the tragic face of his friend, wondering at him again, as he had often wondered, why he should welcome sadness like a privileged guest. And his friend saw the look and himself wondered why Paul should resent sadness like an intruder. 'What's he been breaking his old heart about all the summer?' he thought. 'He's too proud,' even while he loved Paul for never capitulating.

And Paul thought: 'More fight and less power of endurance. He's too humble,' even while he loved Dick for his beautiful acceptance of life as it touched him.

'Heavenly hopes of a moment,' said Gauvinier, trying to find a phrase for his reaction to the poignant words: '*d'affreux désespoirs d'un instant?*'

'No good: "*instant*" sounds like a knell. *Où sont les neiges d'antan?* Such a sounding-board in men's hearts to answer to any beat of sadness! All notes of hope or joy sound shrill or sloppy against the certainty of that drum-beat – *Où sont les neiges d'antan?*'

From this plunge into the unspeakable it was a relief for both of them to emerge, for Paul spotted the cricket bat leaning against the table, and brandishing it, hit a fine imaginary six, soaring well over the Pavilion.

'Cricket's a symbol of life and the world's woe in little,' he gaily declared. ' "With what I most enjoy contented least." I can stand it in terms of cricket. Grief, yes. But miserableness and peevishness and discontent – ugh! Godfrey Daniel, we've got to wipe up Raveley this afternoon.'

'Have we a decent side?'

'Oh, pretty fair! Pretty fair! I'm told Waite's a sound bat.'

'We need one.'

'One or two of us are sure to come off. Usually as long as it's a good game I don't

Paul was admitted into the study, and into the mood of
brooding intensity within its owner's heart.

care a toss who wins; but I always want to put Raveley absolutely through it. I shall never forget it. Wembley, that amiable, lanky ass, benevolent son of a benevolent curate, batting; goes to throw back the ball to the bowler out of sheer kindness of soul: 'How's that?' the whole side yells. For obstructing the field, you know. I shall never forget his look of blank astonishment at the ferocity of the appeal. Oh! They must be wiped up! They damn well ask for it.'

Oliver's grinning face appeared in the doorway.

'Going to have a knock, dads?' he asked. His black despair had vanished, his whole face smiled, provocative, eager, happy, as though no such dull thing as crossness existed. Both men responded to the infection of that face.

'Rather. Come on!' they cried.

'Bags I first knock!' the smiling monster screamed.

'My goodness!' said his father as they left the room. 'The smell of a cricket bat!' And he sniffed the wood's queer fragrance in bland exaltation.

About the same time as Richard Fanshawe's downfall from the study into the garden, grasping the bat, Mr. John McLeod issued from his house into the village High Street, the bulging soft envelope tightly clasped in his small, stout hand. There was a special glow on his rubicund, pleasant face, for he felt proud and important, like a man with a piece of news to impart. It was a hot morning, with the promise of a hotter afternoon. His way led across the High Street and up the hill, a steepish slope, which caused him to remember with regret his adaptability to Mrs. McLeod's wishes in the matter of an undervest. He was sure that he would find Ted Bannister, an agreeable fellow with whom he was on friendly terms, in his yard, as he was dealing with some loads of timber, hauled up during the week: he might, too, see Teddie White, but of that he was not so sure. So on turning the corner at the top of the hill, he was pleased when he ran straight into Teddie White, whose first words were:-

'So you've got the little caps, then, John.'

'Now, how in the world did you come to know that?' cried John, aghast; for having only lived eight years in the village he was still surprised at the rapidity with which news spread.

'Boyle's boy sang it out to Ned, the lad that works for me!'

'Well, I'm blessed! Think of that, now. But you must see them. Never did know Mr. Boyle before his time, and he said to me, plain as I'm standing here: "Mr. McLeod, they can't be done by Saturday," that's to-day. Look at that now, isn't that cunning?'

He exhibited a cap on his thumb and fingers twirling it slowly round for approval of its points, beaming the while with pride.

'What's your size now, Teddie?'

Teddie White was grinning widely.

'You aren't thinking I'm going for to make a guy of meself with a little thing like that on my head, now, do you?' he said, abashed at the prospect.

'We're all going to wear 'em, my boy.'

'Not me, for one!' said Teddie, gravely shaking a blushing face from side to side.

'Everyone wears 'em, Teddie, my boy. Don't you remember the Brighton Police? Every man jack of 'em; and a smart lot they looked.'

'Ah! It may be all right for p'licemen. Look what they has to wear at other times. No, John, my own 'at'll suit me better, I think, than one of them little new-fangled things.'

'New-fangled, my boy, what nonsense! The club always wore 'em in the old days.'

Ted Bannister hove slowly up to the disputants from his timber yard, took the cap without speaking from John's hand, and tried it on, winking. 'A daisy!' he said. 'Just my size.' All three laughed.

'My face ain't made for them little things,' said Teddie White.

'Kinder to hide it, like,' suggested Bannister.

'That's about the cut of it,' Teddie agreed.

Meanwhile John had produced another cap, persuasively, and almost forced it upon Teddie's reluctant head, a fringe, in consequence, appearing beneath the peak.

Ted Bannister shook in slow, deep mirth, and grunted: 'When old John's set his heart on a thing, Teddie, you may as well give way first as last.'

'It isn't as if I always played regular,' White remonstrated.

'Two games now, come, two games and no more have you stood down, and one of 'em at your own askin', when you were wanted bad!'

'He's thinking about his money's worth for that three bob!' suggested Bannister. 'Leery old cuss, ain't you, Teddie?'

All three worthies were standing wearing the little blue caps; in each pride wore a different mask: in Teddie White pride showed as bashfulness; in Bannister as superior calm; in John McLeod as rosy eagerness.

The sound of approaching hoofs on the road caused the caps to be hastily removed; and a business-like appearance to be adopted, as though the three had torn themselves away from urgent occupation to discuss a matter of even more urgent importance. All three were much relieved to know that Edgar Trine and his sister, who now appeared on horseback, could not possibly have observed them standing with their new caps on the grave heads.

'Ah, that's capital!' said John. 'I wanted to see young Mr. Trine.' And he set off to meet him, while Bannister eyed White, murmuring: 'Blow'd if he ain't the limut!'

They slowly turned half round to observe with deep, mysterious relish what would happen. Bannister remarked under his breath with the grave solemnity suitable to the utterance of a great truth, not as generally recognised perhaps as was desirable:

*'New-fangled, my boy, what nonsense! The club
always wore 'em in the old days.'*

'Old John would cut off his backside if he thought the cricket club wanted it.'

'Ah!' agreed Teddie White. 'He would that.'

And they both wagged their heads sagely with the utmost appreciation of John's unselfish keenness and their own recognition of it.

Meanwhile John was gaily greeting Edgar Trine, who pulled up, smiling, to listen, saying pleasantly, by way of introduction: 'Mr. McLeod, our secretary, you know: my sister.' At which John answered cheerily: 'Pleased to meet you, miss. Lovely morning for a ride!'

'Better day for cricket.'

'Ah, glorious! And that's what I wanted to mention, Mr. Trine. The club caps have come.'

Young Trine's horse became a little restive, pawing himself backwards, as though he feared that perhaps a blue cricket cap might be popped on his proud head.

'Steady, now, steady.'

'The club caps have come,' continued John, trotting up nearer again.

'And I want you to make a point of wearing one. All your college caps and so on, I know . . . But what might your size be?'

'Six and seven eighths.'

'Good. Then I'll give it you on the ground so that it won't get left behind.'

The Trines laughed and rode on, Edgar confiding to his sister that old John McLeod was the finest old boy in the village and adding reverentially: 'He can play with a straight bat, too.'

His sister agreed that he was an absolute old scream she was sure.

'You shall have 'em on the ground,' said McLeod, rejoining White and Bannister. That was a good idea of his, that had occurred to him only while talking to young Trine. The beggars might leave them behind in their working-jacket pockets.

'No slippin' out of it!' Bannister laughed: and as McLeod left them to go down the hill into the village the two men expressed their further appreciation of him in the convincing language of wuddy-wuggery-wuck which, oddly enough, they never employed in McLeod's presence except under the influence of the most extreme agitation, and then breath was bated to employ it, as though the last word of truth and confidence made its employment obligatory. A staid psychologist would have no difficulty in tracing this curious use of language, by no means confined to what are called the lower classes, but common to the undeveloped male in every class, to a praiseworthy but stunted effort towards manliness and independence of spirit.

John McLeod trotting down the hill cast through his mind possible recipients of caps who might be met with in the village. Tom Hunter, yes, he'd be in his cycle shop; Horace Cairie – well, there might not be one small enough to fit him – if it were on the big side, though, he'd soon grow to fit it; Mr. Fanshawe, yes, he'd drop in on him. What a man! What a man! and as likely as not he'd find Gauvinier with him: the two were thick as thieves.

There were many cheery encounters before he reached 'The Dog and Duck.' A glass of beer? Well, one, certainly. A capital idea. Never thought of it before. Most refreshing. And the pub just opened nicely in time. Such a well-spoken young fellow, Bob Atkins, the new manager; a thousand pities he should get nasty sometimes. Make trouble and all that when there was no need for it. Wouldn't mind running a pub himself; if it weren't that he could never bring himself to take a man's money for drink when his wife and children . . . He pulled his thoughts up with a jerk. What was the use in harping on such things, on such a glorious morning, too? Oh dear, oh dear, oh dear! Why couldn't people be sensible and happy? They'd not had his luck, though.

He trotted on refreshed and found Tom Hunter ready for a chat, as the morning had become long to him until the game began.

'Such a lot of good stuff in Tom!' thought McLeod as he drew near; and Tom thought, as he watched his approach: 'Fat lot of games you'd get, old cock, if you wasn't Secretary!' but he thought it without bitterness, because he liked playing on a side with old McLeod, though he was unaware of the reason. He did not like to think unkind thoughts; but his sense of truth demanded their entry into his mind; or so it seemed to him, as it has seemed to many others. There was not a jarring note in their little chat, however, and no objection was raised to the wearing of the little blue cap, which Tom declared to be a very good notion. As he had remarked to Sam Bird, they would all get on famously if it were not for this horrible backchat, which he could not himself understand: whereupon John pointed out how difficult it was not to feel a grievance, and how still more difficult it was not to air it, when felt, to any listening ear. Pleased with his chat, old John went on his way to the Fanshawes' house and was immediately taken through the house into the garden, where Oliver was bowling with all his might at Gauvinier.

'Oh, that's a straight one, boy,' he cried, marching on to the small lawn. 'The merest chance he managed to get his bat in front of that one. Good for you, boy: bless me, too, in a match he'd sure to have taken an almighty swipe at it and been bowled middle stump as clean as a whistle. Oh, he's every bit as good as out, boy. So I'll go in.' They all laughed as he came marching forward, beaming and much out of breath; and took the bat from Gauvinier's hand.

'I'll just show you how it should be done now. Come on, boy, bowl away now, and don't bowl at my legs. I'm not as agile as I was. Now, come on, boy, I'm ready for you.'

Oliver bowled – a full toss from excitement.

'Oh, well, that gives me a six, boy: I've only got to tap him into the road and there you are. But I'll take four, as I'm not greedy.'

He had caught the ball in his left hand and tossed it back to Oliver, who shouted: 'Now you be careful, Mr. McLeod.'

'Oh! Yes, I'm always careful, boy. You need not tell me to be careful.'

He purposely hit the nice long hop that came rather hard at Gauvinier and Fanshawe, who stood, laughing, some five yards from him on the leg side.

'If he'd only be as dangerous on the field as he is in the back garden,' laughed Gauvinier, between whom and John ran perpetual banter with regard to poking and wild hitting, as their style of batting varied as considerably as their build. For Gauvinier was as quick on his toes and as lean and leggy as McLeod was slow and short and stout.

'Bless me, now, I mustn't go on like this,' said McLeod, after a merry little while of talking and laughing and batting. 'No one can ever get me out, boy: I always got myself out. But I came round with the caps. You must see them. They're beautiful, nice, little, caps. I had all the difficulty in the world to get Teddie White to wear one.'

He spoke breathlessly, partly from his short innings, but chiefly from shyness; for though at a deep level all three men were united in goodwill towards their fellows, the surface difference due to their upbringing caused old John to feel uneasy and to sweat. With Teddie White and Tom Hunter and others it was the other way about: on the surface he felt easy and at home with them, but he went away troubled in his heart and a little uneasy, whereas after the fret of intercourse with either Gauvinier or Fanshawe he went away with a feeling of refreshment and sureness. He was dimly aware of this himself; and in his groping towards an explanation, had hesitatingly got as far as stating to himself: 'We chaps feel differently somehow towards our womenfolk. And Ted Bannister, well, p'raps. And old Francis. Yes, certainly old Francis.' But he dismissed the idea with scorn. How could he know how men felt towards their wives? All, or nearly all, were decent men. Not all, perhaps, lucky in their wives. That was merely a matter of chance, of course, whether you picked a good one. But goodness gracious! He must check this habit of Paul-Prying into other folks' private lives: it was an objectionable habit and he feared it must be growing on him. Still the number of sick women, and cross women, and unhappy women! Oh dear! Oh dear! Oh dear! It was glorious to see a nice motherly, comfortable woman, proud of her man, with her kitchen all clean. Home, you know. Kindness and well – warmth. Where you felt honoured to sit as a visitor, and pleasant. He could *not* see why ever it should be so dratted, infernally rare.

Meanwhile, however, they had all the difficulty in the world to retrieve one little blue cap upon which Oliver had instantly pounced and run off with. He would like to have worn it all through dinner, the whole day, and to have gone to bed and slept in it. He had not reached the age when he felt it incumbent upon his dignity to hide such emotion as this: though other emotions which men were less chary of divulging he very circumspectly hid.

However, the cap was eventually retrieved, and old John, refusing a glass of cider (he confessed, amidst much hilarity, to his call at 'The Dog and Duck,' a thing, he might say, he never did of a morning), went away. Coming to the cross roads, one of which led to the cricket ground, he felt distinctly virtuous as he turned his back on it and the pleasure of inspecting the wicket, and took the road into the village. It would not do to be late for his dinner or upset the old lady, who would be sure to say he had been overtaxing his strength. If he went slowly, he would show no sign of perspiration on reaching home; whereas if he hurried, as he would be obliged to hurry if he had a look at the pitch, there would be no concealing anything.

Oh, she was right, of course; she was always right, Maria. Think of her slipping out of bed like that and never waking him. He was so lost in appreciation of the memory that he almost passed solid Sam Bird, who was returning with the small basket on his arm, walking still with as careful a gait as he walked when the small basket had contained three eggs.

'Mornin', Mr. McLeod!' cried Bird, his broad face slowly, massively smiling.

'Ah, Sam!' returned old John, turning almost with a start, 'I was just wanting to see you.'

'I should have said, now, you was wanting *not* to see me, judging by the way you was goin' along,' Sam said, making his little point with careful, deliberate emphasis.

'I suppose you've heard that the caps have come,' said old John, wise at length by experience, giving Sam a friendly poke with his elbow.

'Yes, I have heard something to that effect. Very pleased, too, to hear it.'

'Thought perhaps the club might, or some of us might. Sid Smith, you know, three children. Well, I shouldn't mind doing it meself, you know. Don't want to hurt his pride. But why not give him one? Three bob is three bob to some. What do you think?'

'Like you to have the idea, Mr. McLeod,' began Sam solemnly.

'Not a bit, not a bit!' interrupted old John, but Sam Bird had a point to make and nothing could interrupt the making of it.

'Like you, I say, to have the idea, Mr. McLeod,' he repeated. 'But I've lived some little while in this village; and if we was all like you or me, there would be no more to be said. But as it is there be a deal more; ah, that's a fact, a deal more. You must let me remind you' (Sam under way resembled a steam engine in the slow, imperturbable progress of his words) 'that human nature being what it is, we mustn't forget there is what I may call invidious distinctions to be reckoned with. Invidious distinctions, Mr. McLeod. Why Sid Smith? Grant you he has three children and his money's none too good. But if a cap's given to one member of the team, why shouldn't it be given to another? Who's to decide which is to have 'em given and which is to buy 'em? I think it's likely there might be some considerable talk about the matter.'

'Oh! Drat the talk! Drat the talk! It's commonsense and common decency. If you once minded talk, why, bless me, you'd never do a blessed thing. What I ask you, Sam, is – do you think it right? Or would his feelings be hurt?'

'Look here, Mr. McLeod, sir!' said Sam, carefully bringing the arm on which the small basket was hooked round so that its hand was within reach of his right hand and might be tapped slowly. 'Look here, sir,' Sam repeated, having adjusted himself for proper emphasis, 'the point is this: There would be talk; a fairish deal of talk. That talk comes round to Sid: talk always does come round. The talk would hurt his feelings. Now do you take my meaning?'

Sam Bird beamed all over his expansive face, pleased at being consulted and pleased at being able thus clearly to expound his knowledge of human nature. For Sam had read most of the books in the village library, and liked nothing better than what he called a good argyument: and though he was himself the kindliest of men, he somehow felt his own sagacity enhanced when he was able to expose human foibles.

Old John perfectly agreed with what Sam said and liked Sam well; yet the effect of Sam's speech was to make him boil in anger at life in the world and at life in the village and more particularly at solid Sam himself.

'Nonsense! Nonsense!' he spluttered. 'Of couse it's true enough; but it's nonsense, nonsense all the same.' He shifted impatiently from one foot to another, his nearest approach to a dance of fury. 'This talk! This talk! This talk! What 'ud ever anyone do, if they stopped to think of this talk? Bosh! Rubbish!'

'Yes,' said Sam, with immense demureness, and much satisfaction at the effect which his words had produced. 'It's an imperfect world, Mr. McLeod, as you may have heard me remark before.'

Old John was staring down the village street. His face brightened; his anger disappeared as at the approach of a good omen. For he saw Sid Smith himself come lurching home from work; and his coming somehow settled the matter offhand and conclusively.

'Seven, I should say. A good seven. See, here he comes. Sam. We think it decent and right. So there's two of us on the right side, anyhow. We understand each other, Sam. Let who likes say what they like and be blowed to the lot. And there's old Francis sound as a bell. Hullo! Sid, my boy! The caps have come; you must let me give you one. Just to back my opinion you're the finest bowler in Sussex outside county cricket. A born bowler, if ever there was one. As easy an action as old Barlow himself. Ah! There was a bowler for you.'

Sam Bird was heard to remark that it was pitching it a bit too high; when old John turned on him, he said slowly:

'You were always what might be called enthusiastic, Mr. McLeod.'

'Don't listen to that old croaker Sam. What's your size? Seven. Here's one. See – try it on, now.'

Sid Smith, swept away, did so.

'Fits like a glove. Capital. We shall have Raveley beat before the coin's tossed.'

Sid Smith found his tongue and said stiffly: 'Thank you very much, Mr. McLeod,' and, folding the little cap, slipped it in his jacket pocket. It was rather awkward being thus effusively given a cap right in the open street. Old John McLeod had his own way of doing things: meant well. 'I'm very much obliged, Mr. McLeod, I'm sure.'

'Not a bit, not a bit. I wish I could . . .' but John broke off abruptly; his wishes as to what he would like to do for Sid Smith and many others were vast and unlikely to be fulfilled. 'Good-morning, Sam. Good-morning, Sid. What a day for the match! What a day!' he exclaimed with prodigal cheerfulness and trotted hastily away.

Sam and Sid, when his back was turned, nodded at each other and laughed.

'Good old cock!' said Sid.

'No mistake!' Sam agreed with a portentous sideways tip of his heavy head and, turning slowly, pursued his careful course homewards.

'See you this afternoon!' Sid called out as their ways diverged.

'Possibly!' Sam called back, with a wide, expressive smile.

'I wonder, will she have washed those trousers?' Sid thought as he neared home.

His feelings about the cap were mixed. He was pleased to have one; yet, being an open-handed, generous fellow at heart, he disliked the circumstances which made every penny of importance to him; and his dislike of them often made him appear stingy and mean both to himself and others.

'The old swine only gave it me,' he thought bitterly, 'because he knows I couldn't run to one of my own.' But pleasure at the prospect of the game soon carried off these gloomy ideas, not for good, unfortunately; they would always be ready to intrude their grievous presence.

A small person, however, jammed on his brakes and jumped off his bicycle, red in the face and confused at his temerity in thus stopping to accost a hero of his – Sid Smith, the great bowler. 'I say, Sid!' said young Horace, blushing and breathless, 'I'm playing this afternoon.'

'Good for you!' said Sid Smith, drinking in the boy's ardent hero-worship.

'Do you think it's all right?' Horace asked eagerly, anxious to have his mind reassured. 'Of course I do love a game, but . . .' He had been aware of sourish looks on the faces of other boys and other aspirants, who thought they could make a duck with as good a grace as another. Talk, too, of the Gentlemen's Cricket Team, had come to his ears.

The keenness of Horace was a joke among the men; but Sid Smith was too kind to tease him now, and he could sympathise well with the boy's uneasiness. Everyone suffered from unkind talk; everyone hated it; yet everyone indulged their own propensity for it.

'Look here, sonnie! If you're asked to play, and can play, you play. There's a many as would take offence if they was asked to play at the last moment.'

'Do you mean it? What frightful fools!' said Horace, both consoled and flabbergasted.

'I do,' said Sid.

'Then do you think it's all right, me playing?'

'Sure thing. I'm jolly pleased you are.'

'Thanks, most awfully. I say, I do hope we beat 'em.'

'Beat 'em! Course we shall.'

'Righto!' laughed Horace, beaming, and scurried off on his bicycle.

'Oh, Lord!' he thought, as he frantically treadled along to be in time for his dinner. 'Blowed if I haven't forgotten to oil my bat after all.'

Chapter Four

THE TEAMS ASSEMBLE

The Recreation Ground at Tillingfold stood on the road to Raveley. From the Pavilion you could look up the slope to the centre of the village on to the background of Downs which spread away to the right in a beautiful, sloping line.

It was just a largish field, surrounded by hedges, with swings and seesaws in one corner, with a square patch in the middle, on which the wickets were pitched: the ground was fairly level and mown on the road side, along which were fixed wooden benches at intervals: seven in all. But on the other side there was a bad dip and the grass defied, in length and coarseness, every machine but a reaper. Various plans were mooted from time to time for filling in this sorry dip, but they come to nothing, as the Parish Council was not composed of cricketers, to whom alone the matter was of any importance. Indeed, the Cricket Club spent its time and money and energy in getting the ground in even as decent condition as it was; and the football club and the children and others enjoyed themselves, to old John McLeod's horror and that of other cricket worthies, in trying quite guilelessly to undo whatever improvements the Cricket Club had managed to make.

Those who could look a little ahead, gardeners and other sensible people, knew that the present season was crucial. The frantic and costly dressing which in previous years had been thrown down on the square with feverish prayers for rain, would not suffice for another season. The turf, for all its frantic treatment, was wearing thin and thinner. It must lie fallow for a winter under a proper dressing, be sown with good seed – treated, in fact, with the respect that all turf deserves.

'Something's got to be done about it,' said John McLeod and Sam Bird and a few others: but what that something was they scratched their heads in vain to discover.

Football, football, football; the lads were mad about football. In season and out: and the season itself began now in August.

And no blame to them! Off with your jackets: four decent goal-posts ready at once: here's a footer: nothing else wanted. The more the merrier. No old 'uns need apply. Dribble and hack and punt and charge about. Sweat and enjoy yourselves.

Whereas cricket! Stumps, bats, balls, pads, gloves, a net; rolling for a decent practice pitch; such a paraphernalia. And if you were lucky and got a hit, some fellow would bowl at you and make you look a perfect fool; or stand behind you, perhaps, and say, 'Oh, you ought to play with a straight bat,' 'Keep your right leg still, my boy,' or 'Watch the ball,' or 'Where's that left elbow now?' Why, they seemed to think you had to learn how to hold the blasted bat. You might as well stop at work under a cross-eyed foreman as that. Where's the fun of that? Fielding, too. There was a right way of picking the ball up, a right way of throwing it in, a right way of holding your hands to catch a ball. Call that a game! Some were so serious about it you'd say it was a religion.

All of which was so true and unanswerable that John McLeod and Sam Bird and others had come to the conclusion that the only solution was to find a field for cricket, other than the Public Recreation Ground: and a suitable field was not easy to find; moreover, to leave the field so rich with sacred memories seemed a shocking infidelity.

So they hung on, season after season, feeling a melancholy certainty that each season must surely be the last. Of this season, at any rate, there could be very little doubt; the toughest, kindest turf must be treated with some respect: and the turf was losing body. The games were getting better and better; more spectators watched them with greater excitement: the level of the cricket was rising, but the turf was wearing thinner and thinner. Oh! that the heart of a rich man might be touched, and a nice field and a pavilion presented, and the club really put on its feet once and for all after its staggering recovery since the war. What a pity if there was no more cricket at Tillingfold!

But the excitement of the match left no room for such depressing thoughts as these. Certainly they never crossed the mind of young Horace Cairie, who lived a mile outside Tillingfold, and was generally the first to arrive on the field, even when he was only hoping to help old Francis score. Anything to do with cricket was a delight to him: opening the Pavilion by shoving up the heavy shutters, bringing out and arranging the chairs and forms; rolling the pitch. He delighted, too, to help put up or adjust the screens; and to pull the mowing machine, if Sam decided that perhaps the pitch would not be the worse for one last cut. But above all he liked to help Sam Bird put up the wickets, for Sam allowed him to hold the cricket ball and test with it the width between the stumps: asked his opinion, too, solemnly, as one man to another, about the whole performance of this sacred rite, while a throng of kids watched the operation. He always listened to Sam Bird's opinion of the wicket and shared his sentiments fully about the sad condition of the out-field; for Sam always looked carefully round the whole field, and never failed to express his opinion upon it; and upon how the wicket would play, and which bowler it would be likely to suit; and which bowler would be helped or hindered by whatever wind was blowing. What there was to know about cricket! Horace often wondered, should he ever know as much about the game as Sam Bird? And then, of course, soccer! Well, soccer was decent enough to play in the winter when there was nothing better to do; but however any sane person could prefer soccer to cricket the good little Horace totally failed to comprehend.

Some boys were bringing a football on to the ground, and began to punt about near the road; actually on this Saturday afternoon when the team were playing Raveley. Horace gasped as he watched them: it seemed a terrible profanity. Surely someone would come and stop them. He paced up and down before the shut Pavilion, much agitated.

'Swine!' his thought perpetually ran. 'Filthy young swine!'

Similarly, many are outraged should tops be spun or marbles played at the wrong season.

'Thank-you-u-u!' came a cheery shout, and the ball rolled near Horace; who pretended not to hear the shout or to see the ball: he could not bring himself to touch the filthy thing. Anyhow his white boots had dried beautifully in the hot sun, he thought (as he looked at them in making his decision not to hear or see), though they were damp and discoloured when he had put them on. The football was too dry to leave a mark; but he could not bring himself to touch the beastly thing. Oh, good! Here was Sam at last, coming across the road from his bungalow.

'What do you think of that, Sam? Isn't it rotten?' said Horace, running to meet Sam Bird at the gate.

'A considerable change has taken place, Horrie, since I was a lad,' Sam gravely replied. 'The lads have all run wild. There's no doing anything with them. Some say it's due to their fathers being away at the war, and I may say that I am of the same opinion also.'

'But aren't you going to stop them?' asked Horace, amazed that Sam should be making his careful way to the Pavilion, as usual.

'This is the Public Recreation Ground,' he announced, without a pause in his measured tread. 'No doubt they'll stop in their own good time. I have reached an age, Horrie, when I never ask for trouble. Perhaps you'll be so kind as to lend me a hand with the shutters.'

Horace was always aware that Sam somehow gave importance to everything he did; there was ceremoniousness in his slowness and deliberation of movement. Raising the heavy shutters was an opening rite, fit for the beginning of a great occasion. It had a twofold effect upon young Horace, both of stirring his excitement at the prospect of the game, and also of increasing his power of control, because Sam's whole demeanour acknowledged the grave importance of the great affair of the match. His mother's attitude, on the other hand, that 'it's only a game, dear,' the very reverse of Sam's, was apt to reduce him to a state of nervous impotence; and, in consequence, he always begged her not to come on to the ground until the match was well begun – on the plea that the hanging about at the beginning was always dull and stupid; and in the knowledge that once the match was well begun, her attitude would have no power to put him off.

Meanwhile the long wooden folding seats were brought out of their storing place and spread out on either side of the Pavilion (its heavy lids, closed during the week, now open wide like expectant arms). Instantly, swarms of little boys and girls, loosed after their dinners on to the Recreation Ground (while their parents sipped a cup of hot tea in comparative peace before washing up the dinner things), clambered up on these seats, as though they had been brought out and set up for their especial benefit. Sam Bird well knew that this always happened, and he walked carefully up to them in his inevitable manner and spoke to them slowly as he would to anyone else (not because he had any advanced theories with regard to the treatment of young children, but because he had one manner of speech, and one only), after eyeing them a moment contemplatively.

'You naturally understand that these seats are placed here to accommodate spectators of the cricket match, and not to be climbed about on by others: for that purpose there's the swings and seesaws,' and he pointed majestically to the far corner of the field.

'Ah, yes, Mr. Bird!' piped one or two of the elder babies in charge; and the others stared, motionless, at Sam Bird, as though he were a nice strange animal or a queer god or some portent from another world: and directly the spell of his glance and speech was removed, set to work at their serious climbing and clambering with renewed earnestness and vigour; from no instinctive love of mischief (they were too young to have acquired that beneficent sense yet) but from the deep, instinctive desire of self-development, which they were still young enough to enjoy in all its uncrushed force, strong enough to enable the young human animal to learn the perilous accomplishment of walking, and to achieve the tremendous task of speech. They would soon, however, become submissive and obedient and dull, and this divine force would appear only in discontent. Meanwhile they performed arduous and magnificent feats; and the seats bore the strain very well, awaiting without impatience the quiet, steady contact of elderly posteriors, both men and women, which would fidget for subtler reasons in a more secret and, doubtless, more respectable manner.

Gauvinier was the next to arrive on his bicycle, just as Sam Bird and Horace Cairie were emerging from the Pavilion, carrying stumps and ball and cricket bat, to perform the solemn rite of putting up the wickets. The presence of the captain made the boy Horace feel unspeakably shy and happy. All good cricketers liked Horace for his devotion to the game; Gauvinier liked him also because he saw in the boy's unconcealed capacity for worship the first shoots of the lovely power of imagination, which the artist in him knew to be the great distinguishing quality between one man and another. He had said to Fanshawe: 'He'll make a lover, with any luck.' And Fanshawe (never prone to a hopeful view) had said: 'Too good-natured to be anything but submissive to authority.'

This passed through Gauvinier's mind as the three walked out slowly (Horace circled round the two men like an impatient but well-behaved dog), but he dismissed the matter gaily with the thought: 'Anyhow, he's a jolly little cricketer now,' and delighted the boy by thanking him for playing at a moment's notice. The kid's nervousness and excitement were largely transmuted into confidence on hearing that he was worth his place on any side by reason of his keen fielding, and on hearing Sam Bird's emphatic comment – 'Sure thing!' on this encouraging statement.

There was a shimmering dance of heat over the field, and a gentle haze of heat over the line of hills. The square was level as a lawn and faintly marked with the pleasant, straight lines of the mower.

Gauvinier and Sam Bird eyed the pitch meditatively, stepping daintily about on it as though a rich plush carpet were under their appreciative feet. Horace Cairie did likewise. The men's faces were intent and very solemn. So was the earnest young face of Horace Cairie, who was not so much imitative as impressed.

'Should play very well, I should say,' said Sam with sudden brightness, smiling.

'A plumb wicket as it is now,' remarked Gauvinier. 'The devil of it is that the turf wears thin so quickly. Sid digs a grave before he's bowled six overs.'

'That is so,' Sam agreed promptly. 'This sandy soil . . . wouldn't quite do for a three days' match.'

'And these accursed plantains!' muttered Gauvinier, as Sam began slowly to knock the stumps in with the handle of an ancient bat. 'They're bound to spread, too.'

He watched the slow, deliberate movements of Sam, and the nervous keenness of the boy, and welcomed in his mind all the preparations that were being made for the afternoon's game. He liked to think of the Raveley men assembling by their lorry, all pleased at the perfect day, all determined to win or, at any rate, give a good account of themselves. And the little Raveley boys, watching them climb into the lorry, would think their team must be as invincible as the little Tillingfold boys who were clustering up to watch the gradual arrival of the home team upon the ground. And as the minutes of the afternoon ticked by, the result of the little contest would be decided: mistakes would be made that never could be rectified, and brilliances achieved that might never be repeated, and no one knew when either might occur or to whom. One catch in the deep which he had held in a school cricket match the season when he obtained his colours (twenty-four years ago) was still so vividly remembered that the mere thought of it reproduced over his grown body the exact sensations of the half-grown boy, seeing the ball rising high in his direction, running, running, running – would he reach it? – the final stretching, lurching leap – the feel of the ball in his hands, the glow of pride at the roar of joy as he jerked the ball back, blushing, and the length of the way to the wicket to join with as little self-consciousness as possible the congratulatory others. And still, after twenty-four years, Paul Gauvinier, R.O.I., had an empty feeling in the stomach at the thought – supposing he had dropped that catch: and his face definitely flushed at the thought that he had held it.

His eye viewed Sam Bird's bungalow across the road, and his heart desired to hit a six on to its roof. But he dismissed these personal longings with a frown.

'I get too ridiculously keen,' he humbly thought, 'and shout things out that do no earthly good.'

He assured himself that cricket was only a game, but his conviction that it was a perfect little work of art, in which the whole community took part, remained untouched.

His growing excitement began to make him restless. He strode towards the Pavilion at a pace that disregarded the heat of the afternoon – Oh, it was good to be in flannels! – for his bat and a ball to have a practice knock before the Raveley team arrived. Ah, good! here were Dick Fanshawe and that dear old John McLeod coming down the road.

'You can take that blasted football off the ground now,' he shouted cheerfully to the over-grown boys, who were rather mortified that no more serious notice had been taken of their splendid audacity in having ever produced it.

In appearance, which is far more deceptive than is usually supposed, Dick Fanshawe and John McLeod were, of course, full-grown men, one nearing middle age, the other appreciably past it; both in their own way were acutely aware of the world's sorrow, Dick imaginatively seeing life as it is from the standpoint of life as it so easily might be; and John from sheer benevolence for those who had not enjoyed his own good luck: but as they walked through the gateway from the road on to the cricket ground, in spite of their elderly and dignified appearance, they were both in reality shy boys, wondering what sort of show they were likely to make in the match that afternoon. Neither were exactly confident cricketers, and had never been so. Both would have liked, as it were, to plunge into it; to run, that is to say, full speed ahead to the Pavilion, pull off their jackets, and work off their shyness by strenuous bodily effort. Age and wind prevented them from behaving in this way now, and also personal dignity or sense of decorum (extremely strong where men of any age gather for any pursuit), which alone prevented them from ever having done so as small boys.

John McLeod's shyness was increased by unpleasant awareness of his undervest, and he was relieved to observe that young Mr. Trine had not yet come on to the ground. These things were always more noticeable somehow before a game began, or, at any rate, you were more sensitive to their being noticed. But the thought of handing out the caps soon dispersed all other considerations from his mind.

Dick Fanshawe was wondering whether he would have the luck not to get a good length ball on the leg stump, which invariably proved his undoing, if it came in the first two overs. His mind took the conception of the blind spot to abstruse philosophic heights and played with it there, solely to relieve his anxiety with regard to making no runs; a use to which the more diaphanous speculations of philosophy are often put, obscuring the matter in mind rather than illuminating it.

At the same moment they both caught sight of Gauvinier's tall form emerging from the Pavilion, bat and ball in hand, without cap, sweater or coat. He ran in their direction, waving the bat and shouting:

'Coming over, a high one,' and without waiting to know whether either of them desired a long, high catch, he hit one up.

'That's yours, Mr. Fanshawe,' said John McLeod, with immediate unselfishness, gently pushing him in the soaring ball's direction.

'Confound the chap!' cried Fanshawe, dropping bat and gloves and making off with long strides, gazing aloft at the flying ball.

'Five to one on the ball,' old John called out, full of glee. 'Oh, well tried!' for Fanshawe had covered ground enough to stop the ball's flight with his right hand, fortunately a tough right hand, but he came back wringing it.

'Chuck it back and I'll send you another,' shouted Gauvinier, gaily.

But Fanshawe, stooping to pick up his bat and gloves, declined to hear the cheerful summons. He had such a horror of dropping catches in a match that he was an uncertain field; and not all the philosophy in the world could soothe his soreness on this matter. It was embedded too deeply within him. He jerked the ball back when they came within speaking distance of Gauvinier.

'You old fool!' he said amiably. 'What do you want to go tempting me with hand-smashers like that for?'

And his mind sent up the words, *'d'affreux désespoirs d'un instant,'* as he said: 'I can never hold a ball with my arms in coat-sleeves,' and he threw off his jacket, pulled off his sweater, and cried out with much energy:

'Come on; I'll give you a few.'

And he proceeded to bowl at Gauvinier, 'going ones' with John McLeod, as soon as that worthy emerged from the Pavilion, where he always carefully hung up his jacket on one particular peg. Horace Cairie, the ceremony of pitching the wickets having been duly performed, came running back to stand behind Gauvinier and stop whatever balls he might fail to hit, taking off his coat as he ran.

'You won't be wanted there, my boy, not with a couple of fellows like this bowling.'

'Don't be too sure,' old John called back, as, with a look of terrible guile on his rubicund face, he tossed a slow one up at Gauvinier, who, in his effort to knock it through both walls of the Pavilion, completely missed it, to the huge satisfaction of old John. Sam Bird thereupon threw him a second ball, remarking with solemn mirth on the unexpected amount of bowling talent hidden in the Tillingfold team.

Sid Smith appeared from behind the Pavilion, and Gauvinier hailed him immediately, begging him to give him something which could be called bowling.

'Ah!' laughed old John, 'we're much too good for him.'

Sid, keen and happy at the prospect of the game, with his trousers, too, in far better condition than he had hoped, began to bowl, and all the cares of his home life were entirely forgotten. For the time being he had not even been married. He was as clean out of it as a swimmer in a lake is clean out of his clothes and boots, which await him on the shore.

And each man, as he came on to the ground, got slowly caught up in the spirit of the game, emerging, each in his own way, from the habits of worry and care; as each man was given the chance not too frequently offered in modern life of living for a time outside himself, with a common purpose, in which he took genuine interest; and nearly every man, each in his own way, availed himself of this great, good thing, unconsciously, of course, for the most part, but none the less eagerly.

Nearly every man, moreover, in pleased anticipation of a good game, thought how stupid and wrong the constant grousing and complaining were, even while he made mental notes of improvements in the arrangements, which, in the slight reaction subsequent to the game's exhilaration (increased by a mournful, empty day of rest), would be voiced as complaints against present arrangements.

While old John was having what he called a hit, Gauvinier noticed a stranger, dressed in flannels, standing alone by the far end of the Pavilion, guessed it was Waite, the dark horse, whom he had not yet met, and immediately liked him for his shyness. He asked Sam Bird, who, always on the look-out for new members, had acquired Waite's services; and on Sam saying in his guarded manner: 'Yes, I believe that is the gentleman in question,' Gauvinier went up to Waite and introduced himself, both to get him a little warm in the team and also to ascertain for his own directing purposes the right place for him in the batting order and upon the field.

Gauvinier liked a man to know his own mind: but he was constrained to wonder, during the course of the conversation, whether Waite did not perhaps know his too nicely. Number four in the batting list; and cover point; they had a man who always took cover? Ah, well, slip. Unfortunately Gauvinier fielded slip, as he felt he could keep an eye on the bowling from that place better than from any other. He was beginning to feel annoyed with Waite's assurance and with himself for probably doing the man an injustice, when his annoyance was flicked into further activity by observing Bill Bannock, changed, and chatting affably with others, as though no message had been sent in the morning to the effect that he was prevented from playing.

With a mental prayer for guidance (the effect of which was no doubt lessened by its admixture with a mental curse) he withdrew from Waite and, walking up to Bannock, he said in what he firmly believed to be a calm and casual manner:

'Hullo, Bill! I thought you said you couldn't play.'

'Oh, that's all right; my people wired, so I thought I'd turn up in case you were in any difficulty. Wouldn't let the side down for anything, you know.'

'I'm awfully sorry, but your place is filled up now.'

'I'll willingly stand down for Bill,' said old John, whose doleful face belied the gallant suggestion.

'Or me,' chirped Horace Cairie, with a still more gallant and even less successful effort at eagerness.

And of course Dick Fanshawe, always unselfish, began to insist that, as a matter of absolute fact, he really would rather not play that afternoon, and it would be doing him a great service if Bill Bannock would consent to play in his stead. And into the friendly argument came Saddler with an anxious face, inwardly fuming, outwardly smiling a smile that lighted up his rage and anxiety, and said to Gauvinier:

'So I see I shan't be wanted after all: that's good.'

'Of course you'll play. Bill was only good enough to turn up in case we hadn't been able to fill his place.'

'That's it, Jim! that's it!' cried Bannock.

Gauvinier was hard put to it to keep his temper on hearing Tom Hunter remark to

Sid Smith with evident relish: 'Always the same! Muddle, muddle, muddle!'

'Why the beggars should relish any difficulty, I'm damned if I know,' Gauvinier thought savagely; perhaps, however, to see the little difficulties of others helped Tom Hunter to bear his own little dental difficulty more bravely. If Tom had supposed some such thing he would not have been alone in the illusion that help could be received from this source.

The general feeling of sorrow that circumstance had deprived Bill Bannock of a game was quite genuine, except perhaps in Gauvinier, whose instinct, against all the promptings of his reason, persisted obdurately in ciphering up the contents of the good Bill's mind like a column of easy figures. He saw that many vague aspirations had assumed shape and substance in the sending of that morning message, on the childish hope of one grand fulfilment; as though the wish to upset the captain, the wish to make his absence felt, the wish to assert his own importance, and with all, the wish not to lose a game would possibly be fulfilled in one brief and glorious effort; he had aimed his message as a boy a missile at an escaping covey of partridges.

'I know too much,' he thought with sublime humility. 'It's better to take the surface facts than peer into the springs of action.'

And a flash of new colour was imparted to the little drama by the arrival of young Trine on his neat two-seater, whom Gauvinier hastened to convoy away from his father's too aspiring gardener to Henry Waite, just to show what the village could do in the way of a perfect cricketer.

And Waite was pleased at the approach of the two-seater's immaculate occupant; for much as he loved the game of cricket for its own good sake, he was yet complacently aware that one of the advantages of the game undoubtedly was that you were liable to meet nice people – people, that is to say, who imparted a pleasant sense of affluence; not that Waite was by any means a snob, but he felt more comfortable with a man of means, and later on he would be able to mention quite casually: 'Oh, yes, I play for the village occasionally: young Trine, you know, plays. The Trines, yes; very wealthy people: have such a pretty little place near by.' Thus he was sufficiently altruistic to enjoy the mild golden lustre shed from another's brightness.

Their amiable colloquy on the best type of two-seater was interrupted by John McLeod trotting busily forward to dispose of his caps. Young Edgar Trine took one gladly, laughing, and insisted upon paying his three shillings down in fear that he might forget it. Waite followed this excellent example; he also took one gladly and paid his three shillings down in fear that he might forget it. This unexpected convert to a cap recompensed old John for some slight disappointment, barely recognised, at the effect which the caps had produced. They had been for the most part shyly taken as a matter of course; and he had foreseen greater fun and greater excitement. They had fallen rather flat, and his own previous excitement seemed, in consequence, rather silly. After all, cricket caps were cricket caps, and men were men. They were not monkeys to jump about with feathers from a peacock's tail. Still, he had not been able to don his own little cap yet: and he half suspected a fellow-feeling in this diffidence, judging by the hurried manner in which many little caps had been hastily shoved into jacket pockets. Trine and Waite, however, felt no such compunction. On went the caps with brazen immediacy; and Trine said, laughing: 'Feel like a county player now at last.'

And he wondered if Kate really had chosen the best pair of flannel trousers, for a glance downwards raised strong doubts in his mind. And that little fool had certainly not wiped the whitening from the brown edge of his boots. He damped his finger, stooping and rubbed the leather, remarking unconcernedly to Waite, who smiled appreciatively at his unconcern: 'Never can get anyone to do your boots decently. If there is a thing I bar, it is sides smeared.'

Wickets pitched at 2.30, the notice rather boastfully declared, and the church clock struck 2.30 as the Raveley team arrived in their lorry and crowded, after many cheerful greetings to known faces in the Tillingfold team, into the small changing room of the Pavilion, from which loud banter was exchanged with Sid Smith, Bill Bannock, Tom Hunter, and others. To this banter Horace Cairie listened, shyly grinning, and very pleased when one of the team recognised him, and explained to someone inside:

'One of the keenest nippers in the field I ever saw.'

'Ah, that's the sort!' came the answer, which also reached the ear of Horace. 'Can't have too many of them to take the old uns' places when the time comes.'

Horace was so pleased that he was obliged to go into the scoring box to repeat the remark to his friend, old Francis, who was carefully sharpening a pencil, as soon as Gauvinier, who sought the steadying influence of Francis as a cure against gnat-bites (he often said that the quality of the man was as sweet and genuine as the flowers he tended; and Fanshawe, to whom he said it, himself an artist, easily forgave him any extravagance that might lurk in the description) – as soon as Gauvinier went out to court the home side, toss and start the game.

On repeating the pleasant remark Horace got some more of that of which few of us can ever have enough, however august an age we may have attained, for old Francis looked him up and down from under his fierce eyebrows, and, in place of wondering whether the speaker hadn't possibly been drinking to make such a remark, said:

'Ah, and it's true, too, matey.'

This proved almost too much for poor young Horace, who, to hide his confusion of delight, pretended that there was sarcasm intended, and made a pommelling dive at

Horace was so pleased that he was obliged to go into
the scoring box to repeat the remark to his friend, old Francis.

old Francis, perched on the high scoring stool, like a clerk at his desk.

'Now, then, none of y'r foolin'!' cried Francis with much sternness, gripping his small opponent's wrists and, forcing both wrists into one large hand, he horsebit the behind of Horace, who broke away to rush off laughing, while Francis, surveying the group of grinning children, remarked gruffly that anyone who wanted a slap behind the ear knew how to get it. The children did not grin less widely. Children and shy animals, it may be mentioned, did not agree with philanthropic gentry and some others in thinking old Francis quite the most cantankerous fellow in the village.

Outside the scoring box Horace, red-faced and laughing, pulled down his trousers, which had been rucked up during his little bout, tightened his belt and looked round to see what was happening. Nothing was happening. Everyone was standing about talking as though talk and an agreeable loaf were to be the afternoon's sole occupations. He noticed Gauvinier staring intently round, who, on catching sight of him, said: 'Ah, nine! It's always the Home Team arrives last.'

'Have you tossed yet?' Horace shyly inquired.

'Not yet,' returned Gauvinier absently, still scanning the field, which was pleasantly sprinkled now with spectators, and still apparently counting. 'Here they come!' he announced with a sigh of relief, and strolled off to Sam Bird, who remarked, smiling:

'I think it would be advisable to win the toss this afternoon.'

'Ah! that'll be all right,' laughed Gauvinier, and spun a coin, at which Sam cried out: 'Heads.' Slowly uncovering the coin, they perceived that 'Heads' it was.

'You see, that proves it.'

He spun again.

'Heads'll do!' said Sam. 'Ah, every time!'

'Now then, sir,' called the Raveley captain, emerging from the Pavilion, 'this won't do. Practising like this! Mustn't take no advantages, you know.'

'Good man!' said Gauvinier. 'Come on! I was just getting rid of my losers. You cry.'

And he led the way to a bare spot in front of the Pavilion and spun the coin; as it fell to the ground Slater, the Raveley captain, cried 'Tails.'

'It's a head,' said Gauvinier, and Horace ran off to inform old Francis excitedly that 'we'd won the toss.'

To which old Francis retorted with some grimness: 'That's good. But the toss ain't the game, my man.'

'Ah, that's true!' said the Raveley scorer, finding the place in his score-book, and put much bitter meaning into the remark.

'How've you been doing, then?' asked Francis genially.

'Oh, not too bad. Slater made eighty not out last Saturday.'

Francis quietly pulled the score-book over and turned the leaves, keeping the place with his finger.

'Second innings!' he remarked with satisfaction.

Meanwhile Slater, as there was no doubt as to the decision of the toss-winner, remarked facetiously, being on friendly terms with Gauvinier: 'Of course you'll be putting us in!'

'Being visitors, of course, I should like to.'

'I lay you would that,' laughed Slater, and called out to the men in the dressing-room: 'Come on, you chaps. Let's get a move on,' and he jerked his thumb over his shoulder in the direction of the open field, amidst many good-humoured growlings that he ought to let someone else toss for him, that they were just ready for a good sit and a look on; that the time to run about in the field was after a nice cup of tea when the sun wasn't so scorching hot.

Gauvinier called out after him: 'Tea, five; draw stumps, seven, as usual!'

To which Slater nodded a smiling 'Righto.'

The order of batting on the Tillingfold side required much consideration from any conscientious captain, because far more than cricket was involved. As a matter of sad fact there was no steady and reliable batsman upon the side; with the exception of John McLeod, and he was apt to play with such extreme caution that the bowling soon looked amazingly difficult, and his example of caution would sometimes prove so infectious that fellows who were almost sound when they forced the game, began to play back to half volleys that should have been quietly put out of the ground, and were soon bowled by them or feebly caught in the slips: whence a doleful procession to and from the wickets ensued. The whole team would have liked to have gone in sixth, say, or seventh. But someone must always go in first: someone must also go in last; and no one felt quite the right man for either place. The last two men, to show their broad-mindedness, were inclined to take wild, glad shots, reckless even beyond their natural recklessness, in their wish to have one hit, at any rate, before the other fellow got out. So Gauvinier tried to arrange for a steadyish man to go in at No. 7, to give some bone to the tail. Indeed, so far as he could, he liked to sandwich the weak and the strong, the swift and the slow.

A favourite theory of his was that on the cricket field there were two classes of men and two only: sportsmen and others. And in a keen game (the Tillingfold team had many such games) sportsmen composed the side: but the snags on the way to that cherished moment of keenness, both before the game began and at slack moments of the game, were many and perilous; and the atmosphere, when the side seemed composed, for a myriad reasons, mostly of 'others,' was not pleasant – when Sid Smith, for instance, had time to envy the cut of young Trine's trousers, or old John McLeod to wonder on what grounds a man like Waite based his superciliousness, or

Trine to notice and be tickled by the fact that John McLeod wore an undervest, and the whole side visibly to marvel why they had not elected any member of the club to be captain rather than his admirable self. Then quite suddenly some little incident would occur, a good catch, or a smart piece of fielding, which would act on the side like fresh air on a stuffy room, and they would be a team, and not eleven men fenced off from each other by a thousand prickles: they would be a team, and all unconsciously, but all deeply, breathe in the great refreshment that comes to mortals who forget themselves and join in a common purpose.

'Get your pads on, John,' Gauvinier called out to old McLeod, who trotted, beaming, up to congratulate him upon winning the toss.

'That's right,' he answered. 'Put me in to break the back of the bowling so as you can knock it about when they're fagged.'

'You go in first, my boy, to give you a chance of making a run or two perhaps before they find their length.'

A few stock jokes always passed between Gauvinier and old John, of which neither tired; the jokes retained a perennial freshness because, like a genuine handshake, they expressed the confidence and good-humour which existed between the two men.

Thereupon Gauvinier glanced round for Waite, whom he spotted still talking with young Trine. When first Sam Bird had mentioned Waite to him as a sound bat, he had decided that one should be his number, and now he hurried up to him and said:

'You don't mind obliging me by going in first, do you? It's so immensely important to get a good start.'

Waite very agreeably replied that he preferred No. 4, but would, of course, be glad to do anything he was asked.

'Seems a decent sort of fellow,' Waite remarked with a dubious note in his voice, which Trine's genial 'Oh, rather!' gallantly attacked, the public school tradition of backing a side's captain, so far as was possible, being pleasantly strong in him.

'Not an easy job!' he remarked, as they strolled towards the Pavilion.

'What? Running a side? No, I should think not; I've had some.'

'And in a village!' Trine hummed a few bars of a popular song which, in spite of its cheerfulness, seemed to suggest a long vista of difficulty.

As they passed the scoring box, Gauvinier looked up from the list he was industriously writing to call out: 'No. 3, Trine?'

'A little early, isn't it, perhaps, for my glad methods?'

Gauvinier laughed; he always liked young Trine's complete ease of manner; all the more because it exasperated Dick Fanshawe, who declared that it came from an abominable insensitiveness to every other human being. Young Trine was the subject of many a lugubrious homily on the ghastly conditions of modern life, in which the rich took their wealth with a complacent indifference to the fierce struggle for mere existence which surrounded them on every side. But Gauvinier was borne buoyantly over these mighty problems in the pleasant glow of anticipation before a good game:

they stirred in his memory merely to make him more appreciative of the obvious, limitless good temper, that, whatever its origin, was uncommonly agreeable to meet during an afternoon.

'Are people who go deeper bound to lose the mere jolliness which is so agreeable?' he thought with a sigh, and dismissed the thought with a fearful curse at all gloomy reformers who spread their own miserableness until the cloak of virtue, and a laugh at dear old Dick, who took everything so tragically hard. He laughed aloud as he handed old Francis the list to enter into the score-book, saying: 'Here you are!'

'If you're not too pleased with yourself,' he growled amiably in reply, 'you might just write them in the book,' which was Gauvinier's usual practice.

'Lazy old devil! Won't even let me sit on his blasted stool.'

He began writing swiftly, while Francis critically scanned the order. On what might be called 'social' as distinct from 'cricket' reasons for the order, his suggestions were always of great value.

'Well, any fault to find?' Gauvinier asked. 'Come on, out with it.'

A large finger was pressed against the name of J. Saddler at No. 10 and placed firmly on No. 7. Francis put his lips to the captain's ear, whispering emphatically:

'Make more fuss of him. Plant him well in.'

'Right as usual!' said Gauvinier, after a moment's thought. India-rubber was silently handed to him and the alteration made.

Gauvinier went out to pin the list on the door of the dressing-room and, meeting Horace Cairie, explained to him how excellent a last wicket stand might be, and how every run in this match would certainly be wanted, painfully aware as he spoke of the possibility of the last man not having a ball to play owing to declaration or the misfortune of the last man but one. Young Cairie, however, was genuinely glad to bat last for many reasons; and through his jolly young veins beat the excellent spirit of the lines:

> The game is greater than the players of the game
> And the ship is greater than the crew –

which is a good motto for any undertaking, be it cricket or a modest movement for reforming the wide world.

So the final order which Gauvinier pinned with some difficulty on the wooden door in the Pavilion ran:-

1. J. McLeod.	7. J. Saddler.
2. H. Waite.	8. R. Fanshawe.
3. E. Trine.	9. T. White.
4. T. Hunter.	10. T. Bannister.
5. S. Smith.	11. H. Cairie.
6. P. Gauvinier.	

Chapter Five

TILLINGFOLD BAT

The umpires, in long white coats, rumpled from being stored during the week with stumps and old bats and pads in a locker, strolled, great with the dignity of their office, to the wickets. The burliness of Sam Bird had occasioned a rent down the back of his coat which, in consequence, fitted him quite comfortably. As they reached the square, five Raveley men emerged, running, from the Pavilion, and called loudly for the ball which, new and red and shiny, reposed in Sam's pocket; he turned slowly and jerked the ball back to them without a smile. They proceeded to give each other catches, trying tricks which, though more elaborate than successful, were greeted with vast merriment. Staider members of the team came straight out to inspect the pitch, and Slater went from one to another, telling each man his place in the field.

Two or three were seen to be talking to him with very great eagerness, their faces put forward, and the little wicket-keeper, the eagerest of all, suddenly jumped to silly leg or silly point, advocating, no doubt, some deep plot to outwit old John McLeod, whose manner of batting was of old familiar. The little eager wicket-keeper, however, seemed not to have gained his point, as he walked away from the group expressing strong disagreement in every curve and movement of his wiry limbs.

Tom Hunter and Sid Smith watched this little drama with much appreciation. Tom said to Sid:

'They're a crafty lot, these chaps.'

And Sid never forgetting one decision the Raveley umpire had given against him, said to Tom:

'Ah! a bloomin' sight too crafty, some of 'em.'

Meanwhile John McLeod was standing by the score-box, impatiently waiting for his partner to join him. Being very nervous, he kept up a ceaseless stream of laughing talk to all around him, wondering again and again whether Waite would want to take first ball, about which old John was frankly superstitious.

'If there is a thing I hate and detest it is to stand out there and watch the other fellow playin' himself in. Likely as not he'll hit a one at the end of the over and – whatever is the man at? – not ready yet. . . .'

'Of course you must let him take the first ball. Where's your manners?' said Teddie White, gently gibing him.

'I don't care a hang for manners. It's bad enough to be goin' in first with a perfect stranger who'll run me out as likely as not, trying a short one. What *is* the fellow doing?'

A genial cry came from the field. 'Now then, Tillingfold. Come and face it.'

Gauvinier looked in at the dressing-room.

'If you are ready, Waite,' he suggested.

'Oh, I'm ready,' said Waite coolly, as though he was, of course, waiting for his partner to join him in the Pavilion, and rising without haste he eased his trousers and picked up his right-hand batting glove, which he intended to put on as he walked to the wicket.

Old John came bustling up to him directly he appeared, but before the great question could be put, Wait apologised with such extreme courtesy for the delay, that old John's nervousness was redoubled.

Words tumbled out from him.

'I so very much prefer to take the first ball,' he said, conscious of being red and ridiculous before such a perfect manner, 'that, I'm sure, you won't mind if I do.' And he, stumbling, dropped his bat.

'My dear man,' Waite replied, with greater ease of manner than ever. 'Not the least bit in the world.'

'And don't you, for goodness' sake, try any short runs now, will you? I never was good at a short run, and they're sharp as needles in the field, these chaps are; and my wife . . .'

He stopped only just in time. 'Ah, yes . . . well!' he murmured. It wouldn't have done at all to confess that, in obedience to his wife's instructions, he was wearing an undervest.

Small boys and others clapped them as they emerged from the ring of spectators, old John trotting with little steps, Waite walking with perfect unconcern, adjusting his right-hand batting glove. The eager wicket-keeper was impressed by this unconcern and whispered fiercely to Slater:

'I so very much prefer to take the first ball,' said
John McLeod, conscious of being red and
ridiculous.

'They always scratch up some toff cricketer.'

''Tain't always looks as matter, Joe.'

And on old John's approach to the wicket, Joe, who had played many games against him, said: 'Think no end of yourselves in those dossy little caps, I lay.'

'It's the first time we've worn them, boy. The county team couldn't beat us to-day. Yes, middle and leg, please. Pity we can't have a go at those Australians, boy, oh, a great pity.'

On which the little eager wicket-keeper laughed loudly and said: 'That's the style,' while old John rather fussily made his block and uttered a devout but silent prayer that the first ball might not be unpleasantly straight and difficult.

Then he took his stand, treading first on one foot, then on the other, lifting his bat a little, while he eyed the bowler with resolution. The umpire called 'Play.'

Old John felt the eyes of the ten fieldsmen, and the two umpires, cruelly fixed upon him; all seemed eager to dismiss him, with immense hands into which any ball must drop: his bat seemed unfairly small; the wickets atrociously wide and large; far too many people (his own team and all the spectators) were staring at him. Ah! Here it was coming. A full toss, just in the right place too. He experienced the delicious feeling obtained when the ball strikes the centre of the bat – And no long leg! Come on! The run; an easy two; and Waite, without hurrying, calls for the third run as the throw of the fieldsman is noticeably weak. That's a good beginning, and old John, scarlet red, pants and beams and thanks the bowler, while Waite takes an accurate centre, marking a short line with the toe of his boot from the middle stump to the block.

'Just another yard and I shouldn't have had all that scampering to do – a nice four. Dear me! What a pity now! What a pity!'

.   .   .   .   .

'Lucky old devil!' comments Bannister, sitting with his arms on the ledge of the dressing-room. 'He *would* get a full toss his first ball! Give him confidence like nothing else.'

'Old Bill don't usually put down many of them. He's not too pleased,' said Teddie White, who was sitting next to Bannister.

'This Waite chap looks as if he'd batted before,' put in Tom Hunter.

'Ah, he's a cricketer!' announced Bannister with decision. He was something of an oracle.

'Look at the chance for practice these gents get,' Tom, who was apt to be sore on this subject, rather crossly remarked.

'You always takes what chances there are, eh?' said Bannister, who thought Tom slack in attending practice.

'Look at the pitch you gets for practice and all the bats broke.'

'Gor! Look at that. Good old Bill! Fair beat him. Not far off the wicket either.'

Waite had come forward rather late, misjudging the flight of the ball, but he played in a stylish manner, and remained on the stretch, looking confidently back at the position of his right foot, though the eager little wicket-keeper had knocked the bails off and eagerly appealed. But Waite was not easily ruffled.

'Pretty smart stumper!' was his only comment, made with a pleasant smile, upon his rash appeal, while he turned the bat round in his hand to get a good grip of the handle.

'Goodness alive!' thought old John without envy. 'There are cool customers about.'

'Another coat of varnish, Bill!' cried the eager wicket-keeper, throwing up the ball.

'Go on! said old John, softly. 'Not within a foot of the wicket, man.'

'Nearer two foot,' said Bill, quietly, and with a short run and a stolid face delivered the next ball, which Waite drove hard and clean along the ground to Slater at mid-off.

Old John, influenced by the strength of the hit, took two or three steps out of his crease, and when Slater fielded the ball smartly, he was obliged to beat a very hasty retreat, his bat stretched fully out: his natural excitability caused the retreat to be perhaps hastier than was quite necessary, much to the amusement of Slater and Bill and many of the spectators.

'Take it easy, John,' Bannister called out cheerfully from the Pavilion, and John beamed and panted in the utmost good humour, working his little cap to and fro on his head, no doubt to steady himself.

'Well, well, well! Not a run for a hit like that!' he murmured under his breath.

'My call, sir. Wait for my call, if you don't mind,' came his partner's clear voice from the other wicket; and John would like to have explained at full length that he was an excellent judge of a run; but that being impossible, he contented himself by calling back:

'Oh, yes, yes, yes!' and adding in his heart: 'Oh, drat the feller, drat the feller!' to ease his bottled feelings: for nothing is more vexing to any man than to be assumed ignorant of what he prides himself upon knowing.

John was so rattled that he shouted an emphatic 'No' to Waite's summons for an easy run, the ball having been placed to mid-wicket, well out of the reach of the nimblest mid-on. Whereupon Waite remained a moment in the middle of the pitch and returned without the least hurry to his ground, proving the ease with which the run could have been obtained, and John, sweating with desire to show somehow that he really was an excellent judge of a run, leaned forward and called out:

'So sorry. So very sorry. I was rattled and paying no proper attention.'

Drat the fellow for putting him so hopelessly in the wrong.

'Oh, I quite understand,' Waite called back, smiling very nicely, anxious for every reason to put the excitable old boy at his ease; for he was sportsman enough to appreciate the importance of a good understanding between partners at the wicket. Moreover, he liked the Tillingfold secretary, thinking him a game old cock to have remained at his age so keen on cricket. But it must be owned that the unfortunate

Small boys and others clapped them as they emerged from the ring of spectators.

touch of superciliousness in Waite's manner blinded old John completely to his many admirable qualities: Waite's only hope, had he but known it, of establishing any understanding with the excitable old boy was by eliminating himself; and he had had small practice in the accomplishment of the difficult art; indeed, its advisability had never occurred to him. He determined to put John McLeod at his ease by the infection, as it were, of his own perfect courtesy and of his own perfect composure – a most praiseworthy determination – but, as a matter of sad fact, the more courteous and composed he showed himself to be, the more flurried poor John became.

He called Waite, almost next ball, to run for a bye, and short slip very sharply from his fieldsman's point of view, but most unkindly from John's, leaped out at the ball and hurled it in to the far wicket towards which Waite was not too swiftly running. Had the ball hit the stumps, which it only narrowly missed, Waite would certainly have been run out; as it was, his outstretched bat crossed the crease only just in time for safety.

Waite, startled by the sudden neccessity for haste, was obliged to exhibit even greater urbanity, and, laughing in the most genial way, he called out to old John, spluttering and gasping at the other end like an angry turkey-cock with exasperation at this trick of fate:

'Oh, I say, rather a close one that! *I* don't mind a short one, but give me a word of warning.'

'Damn smart, Jack!' said the eager little wicket-keeper to short slip. 'You've fairly shook 'em up.'

And the comment in no way soothed poor John, who muttered to himself: 'Feel like a complete old clown! Feel like a complete old clown!'

'Well run, John! Stick to it, mate!' rang out Ted Bannister's slow, cheery, teasing voice from the Pavilion: and he remarked to his friends: 'It's that little blue cap as is making John feel skittish as a colt.'

Francis Allen, in the score-box, answering the umpire's signal of a bye, remarked to no one in particular:

'It takes all sorts to make a world,' and added, with apparent inconsequence and much kindly relish of the situation: 'The old chap's not half wild!'

'Oh, he seems to take it quite nice. Narrow shave, too,' put in his companion scorer, puzzled and innocent. 'Quite the gentleman, I should say.'

'Ah, he's a gentleman, right enough,' went on Francis, enjoying his private joke. 'That's just it. His rank and stink.'

Too mystified for comfort, his companion forced the topic on to less obscure ground.

'You always rake plenty of them up.'

And Francis, answering the note of combat, retorted immediately:

'You don't, not if you get half a chance! Not you. Look at that for a hit. Just as nice as nice for a four.'

It was indeed nicer even than nice: for Waite, standing fully up, had cut a good length ball on the short side, hard and clean to the boundary past point, who made a mental note that it would be wiser to stand a little farther back to be on the safe side. Such a stroke was not often seen upon the ground. John McLeod's appreciation of its beauty was so great that it almost made him forget what exasperated him in the striker's character. A dogged, sullen look settled upon the face of the bowler, as the ball was returned to him; for he was well aware that, unaided by fortune, he would be unlikely to defeat a batsman of that quality. There was a terrible absence of luck about the shot; a terrible presence of skill and intention. If he could hit a good ball in that way, what would he not do to a loose one? Slater, the Raveley captain, hummed a favourite little tune and put his hope in the queer luck of the game. The spectators visibly settled themselves in their seats to enjoy a display of high-class batting. A large, comfortable, unobtrusive smile appeared on Sam Bird's face and remained there. Old John was relieved to feel that he might play as carefully as he liked while his partner scored the runs: visions of a great first wicket stand shone before his eyes: all the more clearly as Waite took no liberties, but played the remaining balls of the over clean and free, back along the ground to mid-on, mid-off and the bowler.

Young Trine, padded and gloved, and rather nervously waiting his turn to bat, pulled out his cigarette case, certain that he would have ample time to smoke a cigarette before he was wanted. Francis Allen, in the score-box, hastily added another line of ones to the paper on which he marked off the tens – taking them from sixty to seventy.

Old John caught the infection of the general confidence and faced the bowling on the change of over as though his score had patiently reached double figures: in consequence, it was a considerable shock to him when his bold forward shot at the first ball delivered resulted in a nasty little flick in the slips.

'That won't do! That won't do!' he muttered to himself under his breath, as he beat severely with his bat an imaginary lump in the pitch: it may have been a comfort, however, to hit something full and hard, and the unoffending turf offered an impact steadier and less tricky than the volatile, elusive ball.

The next delivery, too, he intended to place between the wickets on the leg side, but once more he misjudged its flight and, much to the annoyance of the bowler, flicked it for a couple towards fine long leg.

'That's more like it, somehow,' laughed Sid Smith to his neighbour. 'We could do that one ourselves.'

'Ten up,' called out Francis, and eyes were turned, heads craned round, to see the first numbers put up on the scoreboard.

'Hope that chap Waite doesn't make a century,' Dick Fanshawe said to Gauvinier. 'Give everyone else a bad heart. He's a couple of classes too good for our cricket.'

'Oh, he's all right!' Gauvinier replied vaguely, not anxious to raise the difficult argument as to who should play for the team. 'Of course I'd rather anyone else came

*Waite, furious, started to run, while the
fieldsmen cried: 'This end, Tom!'*

off. Still, a good man raises the standard.'

'And puts them all out of conceit with themselves.'

'So much the better. Treat everyone as sportsmen,' he went on, 'and there's some chance they may become sportsmen.' He spoke sharply. Dick annoyed him by seeming to hold him responsible for whatever he considered mistakes in the club's policy, and at the same time for running the show in an autocratic fashion. Only friends know how vague small disharmonies can disturb.

But their attention was diverted by the batting of old John, who, having played the ball after his fortunate flick, full in the centre of his bat, drove the next one hard for him towards mid-on and shouted excitedly, 'Come on,' a moment perhaps too soon, for mid-on was quicker on his toes than John thought possible and seemed likely to reach the ball: whereupon John stopped and shouted: 'No, stop!' and stopped: but the fieldsman stumbled, only half stopping the ball, which rolled past him. Waite had turned back. As soon as John saw the fieldsman stumble and the ball pass him he shouted excitedly: 'Come on! Come on! Come on!' and himself came hurtling towards Waite's wicket, at which he was sure that the ball would be thrown. He was behind the crease almost before Waite had turned, and Waite, furious, started to run, while the fieldsmen cried: 'This end, Tom!' Tom reached the ball and flung it at the eager, dancing, yelling, little wicket-keeper, and the ball hit the top of the wicket by an extraordinary piece of good fortune. Even so, had Waite ran at his full speed with outstretched bat, he would not have been run out. But anger and flurry got the better of him; he made no attempt to reach his ground; he ran half-heartedly a little beyond mid-wicket, where, seeing the fortunate accuracy of the throw-in, he turned almost before the ball struck the wicket. His action was a fine public protest against the absurdity of the stupid muddle. His courtesy to poor John, gasping, humiliated and enraged, was unruffled.

'Oh, my dear fellow, these things will happen, you know,' he said in such a way that John finished the sentence to himself with: 'When decent cricketers play with fat, old, excitable idiots whose wives force them to wear an undervest.'

Waite made a dignified retreat, smiling, and answering the cries, 'Oh, bad luck, sir,' which sounded as he neared the Pavilion, with an expressive shrug of his shoulders.

The whole Tillingfold eleven felt rather small, like parents who have been shown up by a favourite child, and yet with few exceptions, underneath the natural dislike of being shown up, sympathised passionately with John McLeod in his distress. John muttered to himself, beating his bat against his pads: 'What an abominable, disgusting thing to happen, now! All my silly fault.'

The eager little wicket-keeper came up to him beaming with undisguised satisfaction: 'He never made a show even of trying to get in. I don't say he would have got in.'

The bowler, imperturbable in good fortune or bad, slowly remarked that he could have made the run easily if it had not been for his swank, of which he had plenty.

'Oh! There was a bit of a misunderstanding, I grant you. Still, there's no need to lose your temper about it.'

'All my silly fault,' moaned old John, not to be comforted. 'Deuce take the feller! I somehow thought he'd get run out. I'd rather have lost my right hand than run him out.'

'It's all in the game,' quoth the eager little wicket-keeper, with a sudden access of philosophy, which did not lessen the width of his grin for more than a brief instant.

10–1–4 the score-board read.

Young Trine strode gaily in to have his knock, as he put it, enviably free of all self-consciousness, for his good-humour, helped, no doubt, by his easy circum-stances, had a solid foundation in his character, which was profoundly amiable. He was healthy and happy and rich, and would have liked everyone else to be so, just enough not to upset his good-nature when they weren't.

His kindly, agreeable, clean face showed no trace of anxiety: he knew that he was a poor cricketer; he also knew that he enjoyed a hard hit, and with a little luck he was pretty confident of getting one or two good ones. If he didn't – well, it didn't very much matter; certainly not enough to bother a pin about, one way or the other. On he walked, wearing no batting glove, grasping his bat by the handle, his eye turning from the wickets to the road – such a safe, convenient six – his whole face on the brink of a smile.

'Another toff!' thought John to himself in some dismay, sore after his painful experience, and to remain sore for many a long day – 'What a shame, too, when I'm not doing too badly otherwise, myself.'

'Middle and leg, please,' Trine called out, and marking his block with one quick tap, stood ready, patiently eager.

The imperturbable bowler knew that he was faced by a hitter, and pictured in his mind, as he moved forward on his delivery, the exact series of balls that would defeat him. No time for that this over; so he tried for a yorker on the off stump, and delivered a yorker, too, which Trine, in his endeavour to turn into a full toss, missed, and which went near enough to his off stump to make the eager little wicket-keeper gasp; and to pass a remark to short slip upon another coat of varnish.

Trine, always inclined to read omens in his own favour, was convinced that his luck was in, whatever his eye might be. Like many an unsafe batsman, he believed mightily in luck, and put his trust therein with almost Christian piety.

It was a relief to the more earnest among the spectators that the over was called at that moment.

'Hang it!' said Gauvinier, 'let him feel round at one or two before be starts that game!'

And young Horace Cairie, almost beside himself, muttered: 'Silly ass! Silly ass!'

'A short life and a merry one. That's my style, every time. No use pokin' round. A full toss is a full toss, first as last,' commented Bill Bannock, in ecstasy of appreciation, and Dick Fanshawe moved away from his vicinity, sick with disgust.

He was extremely nervous himself before he batted, and to see Trine, of all men, so completely without his own bane, and to hear a mad shot fulsomely praised by that lackey, Bill Bannock, was more than he could stand. He could not ease his feelings with abuse – into his tirade, had it been let loose, the whole scheme of things which made a Trine and a Bill Bannock possible would have entered before he had barely started – so he moved away with a look of deep dejection upon his Dantesque face.

Meanwhile, old John at the wicket had pulled himself together in a determined effort to atone in some way, if possible, for his disgraceful mistake in running out a good batsman. He hardly tapped his block at all as he faced the Raveley bowler, and he came forward at the ball when it was bowled with strength and precision.

'Wait!' he called (and the word gave him a bracing twinge) with decision as the ball went towards mid-off, and 'No' he called with similar decision, as mid-off reached the ball and returned it to the bowler. It was another John to the excited, scampering old fellow: this was a controlled, determined John. . . . We often, alas! recover ourselves too late, when the mischief has been done, and we call it learning from experience, affording thereby satisfaction to ourselves and innocent amusement to our friends. Each ball to the last, old John played with unerring precision, and the last ball he put nicely between cover and mid-off for a safe and steady one.

Trine began to feel a faint prompting of uneasiness at the prospect of watching another over after his one glad miss. He liked to keep warm, as he put it to himself, and watching the methods of a cautious batsman left him cold. The imperturbable bowler regarded Trine as his sure victim, and slightly resented his temporary escape. Accordingly he did his best to tempt old John, but without success. Every ball was played safely back, and a nice half volley tossed up well outside the off-stump was left severely alone. So for the last ball of the over he sent down his sudden fast one, which, being on the leg, was missed by John, and also by the eager little wicket-keeper. Trine called and ran hard, hoping for two, but old John was very much on the safe side after his sad experience with Waite, and refused to take the ghost of a risk.

'Oh, no! No, no, I simply can't,' he panted. 'Get back! Get back!' – to Trine, who was dodging temptingly up towards the centre of the pitch.

'Quite right! Quite right!' Trine called out, laughing, well knowing the state of old John's mind at the moment with regard to anything approaching a short run.

'Oh, boy, I am taking all the bowling,' old John remarked happily to the eager little wicket-keeper, who strode up to take his place behind the stumps; but he was too angry at the bye to find any reply.

His pads were big enough, one would have thought, to stop anything; for though he had long legs for his body, his pads rose far above his knees, and his curious lurch from one leg to the other as he walked made them look larger still. His little, eager face wore a most disconsolate expression.

As old John settled himself to play the next over, Gauvinier thought a four or two from Trine would brighten things up a bit. He said as much to Dick Fanshawe, who was sitting next him, and was reproved for impatience: but his wicked wish strengthened while John played the first four balls in his safest, most cautious manner: but the fifth was placed towards long leg, not quite where the batsman intended the ball to go, and a run was obtained. Trine faced the bowler, and took his middle and leg obsessed by one idea only, not on the whole a bad idea, to make up for lost time. The imperturbable bowler hoped that no mistake would occur to rob him of a certain victim. None did. Trine let out once again with all his might, and once again entirely missed the ball, a good-length ball on the off side, which he meant by his reach to turn into a half volley.

Dick Fanshawe, who held his bat so 'correctly' that he was unable to open his shoulders at any ball, uttered an exclamation of disgust at this second exhibition of frantic missing. He was as rigidly conservative in his batting views as young Trine was in his political and social views, wherein some thought Fanshawe was as wildly experimental as Fanshawe thought Trine in his batting, mistaking, you understand, freedom for licence.

Another bye, to the rage of the eager little wicket-keeper, brought Trine opposite the imperturbable bowler, who smiled as he turned to deliver his first ball, happy at the prospect of a few consecutive balls at his victim. Oddly enough, the victim was happy too, because he was anxious to 'have a go' at this slowish bowler, whose guile was not, he considered, of the kind to trouble him greatly. 'Just the pace I *do* like,' Trine said to himself as he took his stand, strung up on his toes for a hit. The imperturbable bowler put down a good-length ball on the leg stump, which Trine, gladly taking every risk, took a step out to, and adventurously hit over the hedge and into the road for six. The batsmen had nothing to do but watch the ball; so had the fieldsmen; and to watch the small boys in shouting pursuit, and to pitch the ball, speedily retrieved, leisurely back to the bowler. 'Two or three of those and the score begins to look funny,' the fieldsmen thought.

'Oh! Good 'it! Good 'it!' Bill Bannock kept excitedly shouting.

And an old, old fellow, who always sat on a bench in front of the Pavilion turned slowly to his neighbour and, creasing the wrinkles on his face in a smile as he wagged his head, slowly, very slowly, remarked:

'That's the stuff to give 'em!' pleased to show that he was quite up to date in his language, and, as though to soothe his own conscience, he muttered to himself: ''E needs be careful.'

Bill Bannock, walking by, stopped for a moment to say cheerily to the old, old fellow: 'That's how you used to treat 'em when you was a boy, eh, Mr. Hodgkiss?'

'I don't know so much about that,' the old man piped back, pleased to be spoken to; but yet anxious, too, to explain, for though he had been able to hit, and to hit very hard, he had always been careful to play himself well in before he took any liberties. He would very much like two or three of the men to know exactly how good a batsman he had been thirty years or more ago – and none did: and there was no crony of his to enlighten them. There was too much kindness and deference to his age in any references that were made to his past prowess.

That six of the young gent's was a fluke; his sixes had rarely been flukes. It was painful to the old, old fellow to be thus glibly misunderstood.

'They don't want to learn nowadays or I'd teach 'em – if I could get about a bit more easy,' he thought, for the many thousandth time. Still, he could, at any rate, see the wickets from his bench in front of the Pavilion almost as well as he had ever been able to see them, and many an old fellow, not so old as him, was too dim-eyed to see more than a mist at that distance.

Meanwhile the imperturbable bowler was as confident of his victim's wicket as his victim was confident that six and four makes ten, and two sixes makes twelve. And this one was a half volley. Here goes! And it went. But not the ball, this time – the wicket. A half volley it was, and a half volley it was meant to be; just the merest shade faster; for the wicked bowler knew that a man who will pull a good-length ball out of the ground for six will nine times out of ten hit across a half volley and be bowled, in his endeavour to paste it even further out of the ground.

The eager little wicket-keeper hurried up, exclaiming:

'My word, that was a beauty!' his little eager face pushed forward in excitement. 'It broke a good foot if it broke an inch!'

The imperturbable bowler did not think it worth while even to put him right: he contented himself with muttering: 'Which it didn't.' And catching sight of Sam Bird's knowing smile, smiled back placidly. Long experience had taught him that no harm was done and much breath spared by allowing people to hold their opinions on matters which could not be put to any test.

The score-board read 20–2–6.

And young Trine, glancing at it on his way in, wondered how he could have been such an ass as to miss a sitting half volley: about fourteen men on the ground could have informed him, without a moment's hesitation.

Tom Hunter kept talking to friends in and around the Pavilion, red and blushing and jolly-faced; far too happy and anxious to give a good account of himself at the wicket to think of his doomed teeth, or of the unfair way the Cricket Club was run, or of the prevalence of gossip in the village, or any of his grievances. He appeared the keen, kindly and very bashful Tom Hunter he was intended to be. He usually came off in this match; it was his favourite match, for some reason, against Raveley, and he was determined to take no risk until he saw the ball well, and then to hit. There was no sense in rushing at it like young Trine. Still, accidents happened at cricket to the very best bats, and he was nervous, and would remain nervous until he got going.

'Let 'em have it, Tom,' Joe Mannerly called out, so anxious that Tom Hunter should make some runs that his usual sauce was not forthcoming. For some obscure reason the boy was desperately anxious that Tom and his boss, Gauvinier, and Sid Smith should come off in matches: especially his boss. If these three came off and the match was lost he did not mind much, and he was pained, even if the match were won, when these three failed.

Horace Cairie, on the other hand, did not mind who made the runs so long as they were made, and the match won, much as he liked several members of the team. In this he was a sportsman far beyond his years. Some queer instinct in him put every member of the side beyond criticism during the game, and all his life he would feel differently towards anyone with whom he had played a good game, and there was that in him which would make almost every game he would play – a good game. He possessed a huge and heaven-sent power of enjoyment.

Horace watched with amazement Tom Hunter's strange posture at the wicket, crouched and stooping, knees bent, back bent, his head almost lower than the handle of the bat, as though he wanted to hide the whole of his large body behind the bat. Most people were so familiar with Tom's stance and play that they took no notice of it. But it shocked Horace so much that he was always forced to notice it with astonishment; and Henry Waite, who had never seen it before, was obliged to seek out Trine, and pass a few comments upon it, after having commiserated with him, not too genuinely, upon his bad fortune in missing the ball. Trine, a Bolshevik in the matter of cricket propriety, and whose good nature resented the sneer which was ill-concealed, assured Waite that Tom Hunter knew very well what he was doing; that he possessed a wonderful eye, and could hit like a kicking mule.

'The way fellows get coached now!' he protested. 'They get all the guts coached clean out of 'em. I saw the last five men of the Kent team batting against Sussex at Horsham, when runs were wanted, and I'm blowed if one of those fellows could open his shoulders: back goes each ball with that horrible forward shot, pat, pat, pat, pat. Twenty-eight runs in an hour and a quarter. Little, well-trained, horrible machines. Stylish as be damned: and utterly futile! Still, I'm no cricketer.' He laughed good-naturedly at his own warmth. 'I've hardly a decent shot in my locker.'

There was no style whatever about Tom Hunter's method. His plan was to stop every straight ball, and to be on the safe side, every ball within half a foot of either stump, and to let the others alone. He kept his eye glued on the ball, and after it had pitched fell across on it, stopping the ball almost dead. A tempting half volley on the off stump was smothered, buried, had the ground been soft.

Waite watched the performance with acute interest; he had never seen anything like it. He felt almost inclined to offer the bowler a pound note to send down a long hop just to see what Hunter would do with it. Yet there was passionate method in the madness: every ball was effectively stopped dead, and the last ball of the over was stopped deader than any, a yorker, which Tom first stopped under his bat and then knocked on his bat, as though to make doubly certain. As a matter of fact, his crouch was so low that kneeling brought him very little closer to the ground.

'Good old Tom! Don't you let 'em get past you, mate,' came a loud and genial cry from the Pavilion.

Which Tom at the wicket answered composedly to any whom it might concern: 'Ah! I don't intend to, if I can help it.'

No bowler much liked bowling to Tom Hunter. His bat seemed to get wider and wider, and if he could stop any ball by that queer means of his there seemed no reason why he should not stop every ball.

Old John always liked being in with Tom Hunter, for Tom, happy as he was happy during an innings, was a perfect companion. A shortish ball on the off old John put very nicely past point for an easy one and a possible two, if he had been quicker and Slater, who had gone to third man, a little less quick.

Tom smothered and sat on the next four balls in the same relentless way as he had done the previous over, and then, for no reason that any spectator could discover, he hit the last ball hard and low, with tremendous force, towards the far corner of the field by the swings – a beautiful off drive – for which they ran, even at John's old comfortable pace, three runs. The bowler was as surprised as Waite, who tried in vain to discover why that particular ball should have been chosen for a drive, and how the shot had been made. He owned himself baffled. The hit was as free and skilful as the blocking was hampered and clumsy. The two shots were in violent contradiction.

Small boys cheered the hit frantically. The suddenness of it sent a current of excitement tingling through everyone. Trine gaily argued with Waite that he saw no reason why boys should not be coached into the Hunter style, to block and smother and bury or to hit. The style had the great advantage of simplicity. There were surely as many sucking Hunters in the world as Palairets or MacLarens or other perfect stylists, whose example we were industriously persuaded to follow. Waite was shocked. He doubted whether even a Trine was wealthy enough to hold such scandalously unorthodox opinions, and comforted himself with the thought that no young fellows were quite the same since the war; naturally, when so much deference had been paid to youth they had got the bit between their teeth. Even office-boys in the city were cheekier and more independent.

Tom Hunter was troubled by the thought of style as little as he was about the doctor's advice to have his teeth removed. His one idea was to stop the balls he disliked as dead as he could, and to hit the balls he fancied as hard as he could. What regulated his fancy and dislikes he could have explained as little as anyone else: the bowlers, in a little while, became baffled and hopeless to see a good ball treated with contempt and a half volley reverently crushed. He had hit three twos and a four; all his shots were surprising enough to be considered mistakes, and there seemed no reason why any mistake should prove fatal. Old John had made three solid ones.

Slater took the ball from the young, fastish bowler, who felt that his luck was completely out, for he had been bowling a good length, yet never felt or looked like getting a wicket.

Hunter was pleased at the change, for he had on several occasions hit Slater in other matches out of the ground. Slater was always a little nervous about putting himself on to bowl, because, though he was the best bowler on the side, tongues wagged as unkindly in Raveley as they wagged in Tillingfold. In consequence, he laughed and joked uneasily as he made slight alterations in the field, and started to bowl before Hunter was ready.

Tom stepped back in time to stop the delivery, and they both laughed and said 'Sorry.' And Slater, moistening his fingers too freely, let the ball fly out of his hand sooner than he intended, a high full toss at which Tom slashed with all his might (he could not very well have sat on this one) and unfortunately missed. The ball hit the top of the wicket, an inch or two below the bails.

'Well, I'll be jiggered!' exclaimed the eager little wicket-keeper. 'Cooh! Lumme! Look where the bail's flown to!'

But poor Tom Hunter was too savagely conscious of having been fooled out to take the least interest in the distance of the bail's flight. Nor was he comforted by Slater running up to assure him that the ball had slipped out of his fingers. That only made his overthrow seem more pitiable.

'I could have sworn it was yards above my own head,' he said, as he made his way towards the Pavilion, hitting angrily at bents and dandelions protruding above the level of the grass.

'I was just seeing 'em nicely too,' he thought and said as he flung his bat down in the dressing-room.

'Bowled by a full toss, then, Tom!' Bill Bannock put his head in to remark cheerfully.

'Yes, bowled by a full toss, then, Bill!' Tom answered savagely, mimicking him, and he remembered that the doctor had told him that all his teeth should be extracted: he remembered that the management of the Cricket Club was disgraceful – a dirty click of gentlemen – and he remembered that gossip was prevalent in the village which was his home; he was convinced that cricket was a fool's game (unless you were a blasted gentleman and had nothing to do all day but practise), and that life was a bloody error (unless you were a blasted gentleman and had nothing to do all day but enjoy yourself).

Joe Mannerly looked in and said mournfully:

'Thirteen, Tom. Unlucky number. Just as you were fair set, too.'

And Tom felt better.

Dick Fanshawe came, genuinely grieved:

'What filthy luck, Tom! Perfectly filthy. We were all just settling down to watch you make some runs. It's a deuced nasty ball to play, a high full toss on the bails.'

'How far?' someone yelled, leaning out of the dressing-room window.

'Twenty-eight yards,' Sid Smith turned round on his way to the wicket to call back.

The figures on the score-board read 37–3–13.

Sid Smith walked slowly, proudly, happily towards the wicket. On the cricket ground he felt sure that he was a man, a fact which the difficult circumstances of his life obscured at other times, for he worked under a skilled labourer and felt, when he felt anything, more like the other fellow's extra arm than a separate entity; and at home – though of course he could assert himself at times and feel a bully – well, at

home he was really more like one of four children somehow, with another expected –
a larger, naughtier child, who made more claims and needed more attention. Neither
at work nor at home, somehow, did he ever feel a man – the kind, good-natured
creature he persisted in dimly imagining he ought to be. But now as he strolled in his
leisurely, rolling fashion towards the wicket, the shouts of greeting and applause sweet
music in his ears, he knew and felt himself to be a man – not an appendage of anybody
else, but a separate living being, himself, a man. He was a good bowler, a safe
fieldsman and as likely to make runs as anyone on the side, with the exception of
Waite.

Gauvinier watched him with as keen an interest as that with which Waite had
watched the eccentricity of Tom Hunter. He would like to have painted two portaits
of Sid Smith – one, the draggled husband and driven hodman; the other, the man in
flannels, a strong, leisurely, good-natured man.

He sighed to think how often human beings resembled flowers out of water, and
drove off depressing thoughts by savouring the pleasure of seeing this one flower, at
any rate, most clearly and delightfully in water, thriving and erect, looking, for once,
as the man was meant to look.

Dick Fanshawe saw the two Sids also, in his own manner of vision, but his face
darkened at the foul state of things which could turn the fine creature Sid was meant
to be into the skulking lout he generally was. Dick Fanshawe never sought comfort
from the harsh aspect; Paul Gauvinier invariably did; the harshness was inspiring to
Dick, who would not allow his vision to be blurred by seeing things as his friend Paul
tried to see them, as studies in light and shade.

Both saw beneath the surface, and the healthy suspicion this power naturally aroused in those who were without this gift was counterbalanced by the trust felt in the other, which went deeper than any difference of opinion or irritation of manner.

Sid knew Slater well. They were both keen cricketers, and each could recognise the sportsman in the other. Sid's natural affectionateness was unimpeded now by any sense of inferiority. He enjoyed the rare pleasure of speaking as one man to another as he asked Slater if he had any more fancy balls in his bag.

'I was keeping that one special for you, Sid, only he slipped out sooner than I meant,' Slater laughed back.

'What sort of guard ought a chap to take against such sort of bowling?' asked Sid of the grinning umpire, who shouted:

'You've got the leg stump.'

'Well, give us centre,' cried Sid, shifting his bat.

He was anxious to make a few runs, but he was scarcely nervous at all. If he didn't come off in batting, he would in bowling or in fielding, and if not this afternoon, he would another afternoon. And the whole enjoyment of being on the field in flannels, a man among other men, went deeper than any wish for immediate personal success. In the same way a hungry man enjoys dry bread, and regards jam and cake as pleasant accessories.

'Don't let's have any trick-running, now,' Sid said to old John with such perfect good humour that his touch on the old fellow's sore place caused not the flicker of a wince.

'Oh, no fear of that, Sid; no fear of that, my boy,' he called back; and Sid made the eager little wicket-keeper explode with laughter by remarking drily: 'There's no knowing where you are with frisky old fellers – being boys again, what ho!'

He became serious and intent as he took his stand, but directly he had hit the ball towards cover the fun in him bubbled up again and he pretended to coax old John to try a short run, who, laughing, waved him back:

'You stop where you are, boy; you stop where you are!' and cover, in the wild hope of catching Sid napping, hurled the ball at his wicket, which he hit, while Sid, leaning on his bat, well in, remarked:

'Not this time, my son.'

Sid hit at the next ball, skying it over third man's head for two runs; and drove the next quite nicely past mid-off for two more, which put forty up on the scoring-board and caused the young fattish bowler to wonder if perhaps his own bowling had not been better. Then he remembered the fortunate first ball and cursed his own bad luck.

Horace Cairie, much as he adored Sid Smith and respected him as a bowler, wished he wouldn't behave quite like that. No one ought to play the ass when they went in to bat, whoever they were, and he thought, in his effort to excuse his hero, of celebrated cricketers whose manners in first-class cricket, he had heard, were too free and easy; how Hirst liked his joke and R. E. Foster was full of fun – or was it some other mythical giant? But anyhow he was pleased when Sid settled down and stopped ragging. Good heavens! Three good wickets down and fifty not up, on a plumb wicket, too, when no side could feel in the least safe under 120 or 130 at the very least. Why, he had seen Slater hit up fifty in less than half-an-hour. Tea, five: draw, seven. And the Raveley chaps could sit on the splice and block, block; it would be just like them to play for a draw. A quarter to four, the time was.

'I say, sir,' he went up to Gauvinier earnestly to say, 'how many do you think we want?'

'Oh! Well over the hundred, you know: all we can get. Mr. McLeod's batting nicely, isn't he?'

'But he is so slow,' the small boy wailed, and suddenly yelled: 'Oh, well hit, Sid, well hit!' but he shouted too soon, for the ball was not going out of the ground, he swiftly realised, but within easy reach of a fieldsman who was making towards it, intent on bringing off a good catch. But he looked into the sun, was dazzled, and though he got his hands to the ball, the ball fell out of them.

'Oh, gummy! Thank the Lord!' Horace devoutly said. And many cheerios came out from the Pavilion towards the laughing Sid and the unhappy fieldsman, who pointed angrily to the sun, into which, however, he need not have looked.

Old John, in spite of the excitement, would not be tempted to a second run. He remembered too many occasions on which a fieldsman, in the general flurry, had retrieved the disaster of a missed catch by running a batsman out. So the home side was one less than it might have been, and Sid called gaily out to him:

'If I get to ninety-nine I shall have a word to say to you, Mr. McLeod.'

'No fear of that, my boy,' he answered, beaming.

Sid was in such good spirits that an insult from him would have sounded pleasant.

Little Oliver Fanshawe, his faced puckered and tense with excitement, rushed up to his father and hugged his leg as though he were collaring him at Rugby football.

'Was that a difficult catch?' he asked, squirming.

'Well, not quite easy,' Dick answered. 'Steady on, old man, with my trouser-leg!'

'You'd have caught it all right, anyhow,' he stoutly maintained.

'I hope so, at any rate.'

'I bet the bloke feels mad.'

'We don't like the word "bloke," old man.'

'Well, you're wrong for certain, 'cos you like Francis and he's just said the very same words: "*I bet the bloke doesn't feel half mad.*" So there!'

And Oliver walked off in the direction of Horace Cairie wondering if he should be able to talk to that hero of his.

Horace saw him shyly hovering near, and greeted him with: 'Hullo!'

'My dad would have caught that catch,' he said, delighted, but in an aggressive manner because of his shyness and delight, and walked nearer as he spoke, every inch a man.

'I am sure he would,' laughed Horace, shyly. He was always shy of a kid when his pater was within sight and earshot, and this was a queer little beggar, though decent.

'I say, I do hope you make some runs,' said Oliver with an immense effort, standing by this time at Horace Cairie's side.

'Look at that!'

'Oh, well hit, Sid!' both the youngsters yelled till their voices cracked, and there was no mistake this time; the ball went clean and hard, with one bounce, spang into the hedge.

'Sid *can* hit!' remarked Oliver appreciatively.

'Yes, can't he!' Horace replied, and Oliver almost burst with pride at being thus for once addressed, man to man, by an actual player. But he was forced to add fiercely:

'So can my dad, too, like billy-o, when he likes.'

Horace looked at the small champion and laughed, puzzled; and Oliver, feeling a kid again, bunked off, turned head over heels, an accomplishment which he had lately acquired, and retired to his mother, with the taste, however, of much glory in his mouth.

'You can do as many of them as you like, Sid, my boy,' said old John, joyfully. 'They just suit me nicely. That was a beauty.'

Old John was feeling absolutely at home now at the wicket, and any idea of getting out came to him as a remote possibility, and not as an insistent likelihood which every nerve in him must strain to avoid. He eyed the bowlers as friends, and not truculent foes, and the fieldsmen as obliging fellows, who contributed to his enjoyment and who were not insidiously active to stop it. There was old Francis marking down his ones in the score-box; there was Ted Bannister, pleased that his pal was making a show; there were a nice little sprinkle of spectators too; and Maria would be coming presently; and the sun was shining beautifully, and he was hardly inconvenienced at all by his undervest; it was a lovely afternoon and a lovely nice game. Just a few more runs were wanted . . . 'What a pity! What a pity! What a pity! I wonder could he have got in? Such a disgusting, nasty thing to happen now. And the first time the feller's played for us, too. Still, it can't be helped. Oh dear! Oh dear! Oh dear! How miserable he does look, to be sure, watching us all batting!'

Both Sid and John felt comfortably on top of the bowling. Sid hit a good three, and John one of his own solid ones, and fifty was put up, which always looks pleasant and businesslike on the scoring-board. Gauvinier's mind was almost comfortable, though he knew from experience the sudden alarming turns the game could take when Tillingfold was batting, however strong the side might look on paper. Horace Cairie settled down on a seat in the sun with his legs stretched out, his hands behind his head. Old Francis marked out another line of tens. A general sensation floated over the ground, somehow, that Tillingfold were pretty certain now of making a nice score. The Raveley fieldsmen began to look hot and flurried.

And Slater, bowling to Sid Smith, sent him a straight half volley, which Sid hit full

Paul Gauvinier, long, thin and sinewy, strode in to bat.

in the centre of the bat, beautifully timed, almost straight back, a low, clean hit; but Slater, inspired, leapt out with the left arm extended, and the ball, travelling at a terrific speed, stuck in his fingers and swung him round with its pace. A lucky catch, perhaps; but the sort of luck which only comes to a man who, like the Raveley captain, has cricket in his bones. An almost audible gasp went round the ground, then loud applause. Every single cricketer on the ground cheered the catch and would remember it as long as he remembered anything.

'I don't mind bein' out to a catch like that!' said Sid stoutly to Slater, in spite of the natural chagrin he felt at being out with a fine hit.

The Raveley fieldsmen thronged round Slater, proud of him, asking if it stung; telling him it would have been wiser to let that one alone; inquiring where he got the elastic for his left arm. And Slater felt the immense joy of having done a thing by instinct; for to leap out at and catch a ball travelling at that pace cannot be done by taking thought.

The imperturbable Stevens, the only other man on the side who could have made the catch, remarked slowly: 'You don't see me putting me hand out to one like that. Not in a month of Sundays.'

'Well, Metty,' said old Francis in the score box to his colleague, 'I never see a smarter catch than that one.'

And the little Raveley scorer, immensely pleased and proud, shook his head, and said austerely: 'He's a fine cricketer, Slater, a fine cricketer'; totally oblivious of the fact that he was a leading spirit among a small band of the discontented who were a continual thorn in the side of the captain, and this from no deep malice, but because he, like many others in Tillingfold and elsewhere, could not see more than one little bit of a single fact at a time.

'Fifty–four–twelve,' Francis called, and several small boys rushed and scrambled to put the numbers up on the scoring-board.

Paul Gauvinier, long, thin and sinewy, strode in to bat, leaning slightly forward, moving quickly, conscious of the little cap, an absurdity for the head of God's masterpiece, a man, but a convenient absurdity: an alert, quick, sensitive creature, as different from Waite or Trine as Waite or Trine were different from old John McLeod or Sid Smith. Sam Bird and Ted Bannister and old John McLeod, like Francis Allen and the old, old fellow Hodgkiss, whose favourite seat was in front of the Pavilion, came from Sussex, and could have come from nowhere else but Sussex, just as Trine came from a good public school and the 'Varsity, and Henry Waite from the Stock Exchange. They could not have come from anywhere else. Even Dick

Fanshawe was recognisable, deeply, tremendously English, with that strange blend of shyness and solidity and gloom and ethereal, essential kindliness – all his outlines blurred like the misty, lovely, irregular landscapes of his native country, that can be found in England and only in England. But Paul Gauvinier – God knows where Paul Gauvinier came from or what he was . . . He was irritatingly difficult to place. The modern artist, vocal in paint or words or music of ill-temper and distortion, found him crude and healthy and athletic. The sportsman felt that he was a queer artist chap; the village people thought him a gentleman, the gentry were not quite sure – was he a gentleman? There were no two stools between which the poor fellow did not fall. He wasn't quite English; no, and he wasn't quite French. He was a puzzle, and yet his keenness made him liked, peculiar as was his brand of keenness. With whatever anyone loved – bird or dog or child or woman or hobby – Paul Gauvinier reacted in sympathy; with the discontents and ills and evils he had little sympathy, unless he could put a strong shoulder to the wheel of the cart that was stuck in the mud. He had personality; and was loved or loathed: loved for the first quarter of an hour and loathed for a lifetime, he used to explain, leaning back with irritating satisfaction upon the love of a few staunch friends.

The sunshine and a good game of cricket! He was acutely aware of both and immensely happy, and a thousand other awarenesses touched him; little vibrations from the children and spectators; the line of the hills; the softness of the grass; the feel of his flannels; the throbbing longing to make some runs; the state of the match; the pleasure of Slater in holding Sid's hit; Sid's sickness in being out; old John's satisfaction in his prolonged stay at the wickets; how cricket brought old and young, rich and poor, good and bad, together for a time; the eager little wicket-keeper's earnest, tight little face; the women and the girls, and the soaring swallows, and the sadness and dreariness and the gleams of light and joy – it all flowed on and was merged in the sunshine, so hot and still, and a good game of cricket. He smiled as he strode in to bat, feeling the luck of the game had swung round for the moment against Tillingfold, alert to swing it back, and deep down within him nervous as a kid, nervous as when he first went in to bat for the school, a little boy among big boys or men; and enjoying this sense of being a child again. Impatient, of course, impatient and fretting to be at it, every nerve stretched and quivering like a race-horse, eyes bright, nostrils stretched, the queer creature, for all the artist and the Frenchman in him, yet had cricket in his bones, even as Sid Smith or Henry Waite or the old, old fellow Hodgkiss – or little Oliver Fanshawe, or Horace Cairie for that matter, though these children could hardly be said to have formed their bones yet.

There was one ball to play in the over, a good-length ball, which glanced off his leg for what was a safe run even for his stout and breathless friend. Slater knew that his blind spot in the first two overs was a good-length ball on the leg stump, and came within a few inches of giving him one: a less sportsman-like bowler would have uttered a loud appeal for leg before wicket; as it was, the little wicket-keeper, out of sheer eagerness, uttered a cry which might have been mistaken for an appeal. He distracted attention from it by asking the umpire to signal a leg bye before the umpire had had time to do so. The umpire, annoyed, paid impressive disregard to his eagerness; and the little man tried to work off his squashed feeling by informing Gauvinier in confidence, after he had crossed over, how often the umpire forgot to signal leg byes.

The imperturbable Stevens usually bowled with the accuracy of a machine, putting the ball within an inch or two of the spot on which he desired it to pitch. If you watched him carefully his bowling presented few insuperable difficulties: he was a safe and tireless bowler. But in his anxiety to put down an extra fast ball without changing his run or his action, he bowled a ridiculous long hop which pitched well out on the off-side and, striking the edge of a new turf, put in to fill an old block, shot up and across at Gauvinier's head. Had Gauvinier been wise and not impatient, he would have stopped and let the thing severely alone; but in the crucial second of decision he saw the ball lifted nicely out into the road, swung his bat at it, misjudged its pace and flight, and flicked it towards slip, who, jumping, smacked the ball with his hand, and the eager little wicket-keeper, his eagerness at last repaid, turning and yelling: 'I'll have it,' fell forward and held it in his sticky, gloved hands, rolling over, hands up, not because he could not stop himself from rolling, but simply to finish it off in style, from exuberance.

Raveley luck was still in, and Gauvinier was well out, as surely as if he had been bowled middle stump by a beauty or caught in the long field off a clean high hit.

Old Francis in the score-box, referring to the Raveley luck, remarked in an undertone: 'Oh, damn it, that's a bit too stiff' and called out in a stern voice:

'Total, fifty-one, wickets, five; last man, nought.'

But again, lucky as the catch was, the luck could not have have happened to a fielding side that was not sharp as knives, on the tips of their toes, eyes skinned to snap a chance.

Ten minutes ago, with Sid Smith nicely set and Gauvinier to bat, and fifty sitting pleasantly on the board, Tillingfold looked in a comfortable position; now with Sid Smith and Gauvinier out, either of them capable of making runs quickly, matters looked serious for Tillingfold. Of course, the tail might wag, but it might not; on one occasion, when five wickets had fallen for eighty-six, the whole side had failed to reach ninety. Stevens and Slater could work havoc with a tail. Anything might happen.

'Great Goodness!' thought Horace Cairie, 'we shan't reach seventy-five at this rate, let alone the century.'

And he felt sick in the stomach.

.   .   .   .   .

Jim Saddler had not expected the swift downfall of Sid Smith and of Gauvinier; in consequence he was buckling on his first pad when Gauvinier returned to the changing-room. And, being in a hurry and very nervous and excited, he fumbled the straps and cursed softly and could not find the fellow to the pad he at last did put on. Sid Smith came to the rescue; found and buckled on the second pad for him, otherwise what with stooping (for he was shortish and very thick) and what with anger (for he was very hot-tempered) and what with nervousness (for he was shy and excited as any boy), Jim Saddler would probably have broken some small blood-vessel in his neck or cheeks.

'And any that come at your face, Jim, you duck your head to 'em,' said Sid, having a gentle knock at Gauvinier, who was wise enough not to express his feelings either about the delay or his dismissal, in words; never realising how expressive was the look of his tell-tale face, which doubled poor Jim Saddler's nervous flurry.

At last a bat was found, and Jim, ready, hastened off, stumbling down the steps, ignoring Gauvinier's remark that there was no need to hurry.

'Might as well knock his wicket down at once for all the good he is in that state,' Gauvinier thought savagely.

But all his fury burst and passed off in merriment at the sight of thick Jim Saddler making his way to the wicket with little runs between his strides. For Jim had the largest behind of any man in Sussex, and must have had trousers specially built for it. If only he could sit in front of the wicket, the match would be saved. No ball could pass that immense protection. The bat looked like a child's toy in his grasp, and a shy child looked out of his blue eyes, in spite of his proportions and his bushy moustache and his imposing manner of maintaining what he considered to be his rights as a man.

Jim Saddler was a desperately keen cricketer, with grit in him, and a fine appreciation of the game, but a cricket bat in his hands did not seem to be the weapon best suited to deal with a moving ball. It seemed, moreover, to turn his arms and wrists into its own uncompromising wood. But there was something dogged about him, and he never budged from his stance, however the ball might be bumping.

Stevens thought that a yorker on the middle stump would about do for him, and gave him a nice one, which probably would have bowled him had he lifted his bat, but he did not raise his bat more than an inch, then pressed heavily on the handle and let the ball hit the bat. That was his method of 'playing,' and though it was ungraceful, it was at times effective, for any ball on the wicket was treated in this way. Any ball off the wicket he hit; and he had one method of hitting, and one only – a sort of scoop or swing round to leg, which, owing to the immense strength of his arms, made runs.

The fifth ball of the over came straight at his body. Jim, steady on his feet as a rock, swung his bat round and scooped it for two, both short men running their very best between the wickets, keenly aware of the importance now of every run.

Shouts of applause greeted the hit and the running, for the spectators were fearing a rot, and were given hopes by the hit that a rot might still be averted. There was more excitement now in the match than there had ever been. Small boys chanted out, '*Play up, Tillingfold! Play up, Tillingfold!*' to a low, rhythmical catch, and many players and grown men took it up, and it sounded most impressive. It broke into the cries of 'Good old Jim!' 'Well hit, mate,' when Jim's stiff swing at Stevens' fast one flicked the ball to long leg for two more – a mis-hit; but mis-hits count, and annoy even the most imperturbable bowler.

Jim Saddler was boiling with excitement and delight; his cheeks gleamed and shone; his blue eyes danced. He might not be worth asking to play until the very last moment, but, damn it! he was doing better than some he could mention, for all that. It wasn't always the best ones as made runs when runs were wanted. And that conceited, swaggering gasbag, Bill Bannock, wasn't half mad at watching him making runs. He might be smarter behind the stumps and have more stuff to put on his ground – still, there were others as could make a run or two when they were wanted; and it was a blasted good thing that old Bill should know it, and know, too, that there were other pebbles on the beach besides him.

The shouting and excitement stiffened John McLeod's resolution to play the game of his life, in spite of the disastrous opening of his innings. He felt the delighted sensation of rising to an emergency; and the delight of the sensation was by no means lessened by his consciousness that he was partly responsible for the emergency's existence.

> Our past is clean forgot
> Our present is and is not
> Our future's a sealed seed plot –

the poet correctly states, though he was not thinking of the Tillingfold Cricket Team in its match against Raveley.

There was no wobbling or uncertainty about John's batting; the ball found the centre of the bat each stroke, and though Slater was bowling well, he never looked like getting John out, and the maiden over was greeted with cheers, a rare thing on the Tillingfold ground, and a thing which gratified John intensely, because he often thought a little sadly that his batting, because he did not slog wildly and make showy hits for six, was not properly appreciated.

But a jolt came against his sense of gratification. Surely some imp of mischief must have been hovering round the field, intent to play pranks on John's conviction that he was a judge of a run, which he quite assuredly was. For Jim Saddler, swept away by excitement, made his scoop and started running without the hint of a call, and John ran too, anxious, not to stand on his rights, but to avoid being even the innocent cause of another man's getting out. Then, as they were about to meet in the middle of the pitch, Jim took fright, yelled 'Get back,' and bolted for his own wicket, and old John yelled 'Come on now you've started,' and most of the fieldsmen yelled 'This end,' and Jim turned and started running back towards the centre of the pitch just as John started for his own wicket . . . and the man with the ball, had he lobbed to either end, would have run either man out, but, caught in the general confusion, he hurled the ball at John's wicket with all his might, and missed it by yards, which John, seeing, turned once more, summoning Jim for the overthrow, who, distraught, stood gaping inside his crease. 'Aren't you coming? Aren't you coming?' cried John, but Jim would not or could not speak or move, and old John turned yet again, and again the man with the ball had only to lob at the wicket to run him easily out, but in his furious anxiety hurled it high and hard and old John was saved. He stood panting, breathless, rattled, leaning on his bat, listening to the shouts of laughter and the cries that he could walk an easy run now.

'Oh dear! Oh dear! Oh dear!' he good-naturedly wailed, 'all that terrible racing and rushing about for nothing. What a ass of a fellow! What a ass of fellow, now, to be sure!'

And he felt certain that Waite was watching and enjoying and misjudging, and to be misunderstood is painful at any age. Oh, he could have explained it all; he could have explained it all right enough if he only got the chance and were articulate!

Waite, indeed, was receiving some comfort and much amusement from the exhibition. He remarked to Trine, by whose side he was comfortably settled on a backed seat: 'If only those chaps could be taught to run decently. That's where a certain amount of coaching is ab-so-lutely necessary. Always say something. Always back up. To know whose call it is – it's got to be in your bones; I suppose it can't be learned at that age. It was driven into me at the prep. Oh, earlier! I simply drank it with my mother's milk.'

'Of course there is a lot to be learned in cricket,' Trine assented. 'Far more than people who *don't* know realise. It's not all genius and sweet will.'

'I wouldn't have missed it for anything to see those fat little chaps bucketing about in the middle of the pitch.'

The little fat chaps had regained their breath and were reaching out after their steadiness, which the scramble had shaken. Jim Saddler planted his bat firmly for the next two balls to break against as waves break against a groyne. He scooped strongly at the next and flicked it for a safe one; and John made his best shot off the next between cover and point for another. The score was slowly mounting towards sixty. Then Jim had an inspiration and a triumph. He actually moved out of his ground at the last ball of the over, swung his bat round with immense force and, to his own glee and the delight of the spectators, banged an unmistakable four to the leg boundary.

Stevens, imperturbable as he was, breathed a quiet, unspoken curse that it happened to be the last ball of his over, confident that he would have had Saddler nicely on top of that lucky pull.

Jim did not consider the four 'a lucky pull': he considered it a well-timed, well-placed hit, which he hoped that Bill Bannock saw. He felt a batsman, pure and simple; and decided that he was not scratching and scrambling after an odd run or two, but in for a good, steady display of batting. His nerves began to vibrate less tensely. He took the run when John flicked Slater to long leg, as though any muddle in running could not happen when he was at the wickets. He stopped four of Slater's deliveries without overbalancing himself in the least, and Slater, becoming impatient at good bowling taking so little effect, thought he would try a lark and send him a high, full toss – which he did. Alas for poor Jim Saddler! He had no means of defence or attack with such a ball. He waved his bat at it, rather as though he were trying to reach a high twig with a swophook, somehow hit it – a 'lolly' into the hands of point.

Partly for having stopped a rot, partly for the amusement he had given, Jim received a small ovation on returning to the Pavilion, which compensated him for getting out in that foolish manner just as he felt he was in for a good innings.

Waite annoyed Trine by putting to him, as a sort of problem, the answer to which it would be interesting to know, how many runs in a match like this were made by hits anywhere in the direction the batsman intended, and how many players either got themselves out or were got out by the worst balls.

Dick Fanshawe, in pads and gloves, overheard this remark, and would have liked to crack Waite's head with his cricket-bat in the wild hope that he'd let some of the superciliousness out and a little something else in. His anger at Waite's talk was almost greater than his nervousness at the prospect of batting. He looked, scowling, at the score-board – 62–6–9 – Tillingfold were by no means out of the wood yet.

'Now just you stop out there till I put the hundred up,' called out Francis from his stool in the score-box.

'Ah! Shouldn't I like to, Francis!' Dick answered, smiling. He was always pleased when Francis Allen spoke to him.

Jim Saddler was explaining to Bill Bannock, in the most friendly manner, that he could play the good ones all right, but it was deuced odd he simply did *not* know what the hell to do with the silly thing that got him out: while he wiped his face, rosy and shiny as a licked, rubbed apple, with a very large pocket-handkerchief, and Bill Bannock listened, amiably grinning, and agreeing, and taking many notes for future derisive comment upon poor old Jimmie Saddler.

Dick Fanshawe went to the wicket in much the same spirit of lofty resignation as a martyr went to the stake. He enjoyed cricket, but there was nothing light-hearted or flippant in his enjoyment. No vision of the ball soaring beautifully into the road flickered before his stern grey eye. On the contrary, so resolved was he to avoid the temptation of hitting too soon or too hard, that he would be set like cement before treating the sweetest long hop on the leg with disrespect or even the juiciest full toss. One might have thought that the temptation not to hit wildly would be lessened by the fact that he habitually held his bat with such grim correctness that he could not hit at all; but that was not the case. Gauvinier often thought he held himself with the same harsh correctness with which he handled his bat, gripping himself with a fierce sense of duty, as though a moment's relaxation would have shocking results. They may have had: no man can answer for another; but his friend, having often felt his delicate sensitiveness, wondered whether such grim treatment was quite necessary, just as he wondered whether a less tightly correct grip on the bat handle would not have freed his great strength for action. He had suggested the latter possibility at practice, but the suggestion was sadly countered by the undoubted truth that a good hit was the result of correct timing rather than of mere brute strength.

It was as though the racer had taken his code and his standard from the cart-horse; for out of the plodding tenacity shone perpetual gleams of spirit and of pace.

'It won't be for want of trying, if he does get out,' Gauvinier heard Sid Smith remark with a touch of defiance at anyone who might be fool enough not to realise the truth of what he said: and with the same note of defiance he added: 'I reckon no one in Tillingfold's keener on cricket than Mr. Fanshawe, and no one can do more than his best.'

As Dick Fanshawe took his stand at the wicket, even though John McLeod was to play the ball, the game took on a more serious character. Even the small boys in the surrounding half-moon of spectators felt this change of atmosphere.

'Oh, Lord!' thought Gauvinier in anguish, 'what's it matter if the old darling does take a nought? After all, cricket's only an idiotic game: knocking a leather ball about with a wooden bat.'

But this was only a feeble struggle before he was sucked into the painful tenseness of the occasion.

'No! rang out Dick's hollow voice. 'Stay where you are, Mr. McLeod!'

The game took on tremendous purpose. Old John's rubicund countenance tried its utmost to assume an austere aspect. Gauvinier thought, with a sigh, that Dick would never be really happy until he had taken one glad, unthinking smite and the smite had come off, the bat taking the ball on the beautiful right place that seems to give wings to the tough, round, leather ball. The profanity, however, hurried off and away out of his mind, like a naughty child escaping from a room full of elderly persons.

The captain in him thought gloomily: 'It's all right, of course, but we want runs,' even while the friend in him wished with all his heart that Dick might stay at the wicket for hours.

Now Fanshawe was facing Slater after John had played a careful maiden from the imperturbable Stevens, who knew exactly where he was in bowling to that careful bat: it was a question, really, which would tire first, and Stevens knew that he never tired: good-length ball followed good-length ball with unwearying precision and was met with a reverent straight bat, as though machine faced machine. It did not seem that runs could ever be made at cricket. Nor did the likelihood of runs increase appreciably while Fanshawe faced Slater. The first two balls were conscientiously directed back towards mid-off and mid-on respectively, but he faltered at the third ball and snicked it by mistake past short slip and John called for and took a run, to which Fanshawe responded almost against his will, as though to take a run off such a shot were a base deed. The steadiness of the batsmen had its influence on Slater, and put him up to tricks which Stevens would never have played. He thought to disconcert old John by sending him a slow, straight, high-tossed, full pitch, such as had proved the downfall of Jim Saddler; but the full pitch was not tossed quite enough and did not come quite straight enough and old John, timing the ball nicely, despatched it for a comfortable two, in spite of the length of grass in that portion of the ground over which the ball was asked to travel. The hit shook up Slater, and the next ball he sent down was a really good one which come in from the off and missed the bail of the leg wicket by the fraction of an inch.

'Didn't know much about that one, boy,' said old John, beaming at not being bowled. 'And it couldn't have been very far from the wicket.'

'Another coat of varnish,' the eager little wicket-keeper grumbled, bringing out his favourite comment, in a tone that inferred, without much justification, that the Raveley players were struggling against atrocious ill-luck.

'Ah, well!' laughed old John, uncowed, 'a miss is as good as a mile any day.'

The next ball, well on the leg side, John missed, and the eager wicket-keeper crossly kicked at it rather than got behind it, and kicked it for one: whereupon the schoolmaster explained to some little pupils by his side that a leg-bye was a bye that came off the wicket-keeper's pads on the on side. The small rustic cricketer has many difficulties with which to contend in acquiring a knowledge of the noble game of cricket, even as the small public schoolboy (Gauvinier, who heard the remark with glee, was quick inwardly to add) with the nobler art of life.

Slater, by a strange flight of fancy, thought Fanshawe might be tempted; but the half volley widish on the off was driven back austerely along the carpet towards mid-off (as a grave, good man might decline the most laughing invitation to a kiss). Waite and Gauvinier and Tom Hunter and young Trine all wished in their hearts with a sudden ache of longing that they were still at the wicket when fours were being thus generously offered. And Jim Saddler, still elate from his display, remarked hoarsely: 'I'd have like to give that one a punch.' At which Sid Smith shook his head sagely and said: 'You won't never see Dick Fanshawe takin' no liberties.' And Gauvinier bit his lip to keep himself from shouting out: 'Let 'em have it!' If you didn't hit a ball like that, hang it, what ball could you make runs off? It was an unkind question to put, even in thought.

Slater, reckless, took a longer run and tried to bowl a faster ball than he had ever bowled in his life, to york Fanshawe's leg stump clean out of the ground: it was a yorker, and very fast, but Fanshawe touched it with the edge of his bat and it went for two runs.

Anyhow, runs came 'somehow or other how,' as Francis in the score-box smiling said to his angry colleague, who retorted:

'That's what fair gets up my sleeve, just when they should finish it off they doesn't, and the score creeps up and creeps up.'

'Ah, that's cricket all over, mate,' Francis answered, soothing him. 'This is a ding-dong game, this is.'

'Get Slater setting about it and he'll give you ding-dong,' and he broke the lead of his pencil which he was sharpening, by no means to be soothed.

Maria McLeod came on to the ground, passing discreetly, as was her wont, along the road and in at the far gate by the Pavilion, behind which she made her modest way, as usual, a little surprised, as she knew that Tillingfold were batting, not to be met by her husband at the gate. She could not see, being rather short, over the hedge by the road, and she was too shy to peer in at the small gate midway. She was in her best clothes; when she came to watch a cricket match she liked to do the thing, as she considered, properly, and not to put herself forward in any way because her husband happened to be Secretary of the Club. She felt the little nip in the wind as she walked, and was relieved to think that dear John was wearing his little undervest. Such nonsense to mind what foolish young people thought or said about anything so very sensible as wearing an undervest. It would surely be more gentlemanly not to notice what underclothing anyone was wearing than to pass remarks. She looked about everywhere for her husband, and the last place she thought of looking for him was at the wicket. She usually arrived late, and John batted early, and his stay at the wicket was not prolonged as a rule: indeed, one reason of her late arrival was her dread of seeing John struck by the horrid hard ball, for she knew that he was soft in places and wasn't as young as he was. She kept her eyes, however, from wandering too freely in case she might too suddenly catch sight of John or Mr. Bannister in their little blue caps and be moved to an unseemly exhibition of mirth. As it was, the memory of John in bed that morning wearing his little blue cap caused her to clear her throat with much care. Oh, dear! Here was Mr. Gauvinier coming up to her!

'Looking for your husband, Mrs. McLeod?' said Paul. 'Why, he's at the wicket; playing the game of his life.'

'You don't mean to say he's been running about out there in the sun all the afternoon?'

'Yes, he's been batting magnificently.'

'And he'll have to stand fieldsman after he's had his tea?'

'Oh, yes.'

'Then, Mr. Gauvinier, I must ask you to stop him now,' she said very shyly.

'Stop him now?'

'From overtiring himself, running about with them pads on and the bat; and I am not sure that little blue cap is sufficient protection from the sun, and he'll be that hot, poor soul. . . .'

It was as shocking, with Fanshawe at the wicket, to hear a woman speak in this desecrating manner as to hear a girl whistle in church when an archbishop stood in the pulpit. The captain knew that the secretary's wife, like many other excellent women, was not up to all the niceties of cricket, but he did not know that her ignorance was as abysmal as this.

'It must be more fatiguing to run about with them pads and carrying a bat than to run about without them. You are the captain and can declare him stopped.'

'Oh, my dear Mrs. McLeod . . . you don't know what your husband would say. He'll never forget it if he carries his bat through the innings. This is a great occasion.'

'Well, Mr. Gauvinier, I am sure you will pardon me, but I do think that a man's health is of more importance than any game.'

Gauvinier suddenly realised that Mrs. McLeod's attitude was precisely the same as that of a mother watching her son among other little children playing in the street. There was no difference at all in her mind between one game and another. She answered, 'Yes, dear; yes, yes,' to the explanations of her son with regard to the beauties of 'Last Across,' as she would answer, 'Yes, dear; yes, yes,' to John's description of his innings or of the match – with the same tolerant, kindly indifference to what was said and the same alert eye for the physical state of the speaker.

Mrs. McLeod was saying in a hesitating, embarrassed voice: 'He is a stoutish man . . . in front, and that ball is very hard and . . .'

To ease her mind Paul led her to a backed chair (the backed chairs were a pride of Sam Bird and the Cricket Club, specially for the accommodation of ladies, you understand, for we cricketers like our womenfolk to watch our prowess even when the ladies are not gifted with an intelligent appreciation of the game: we feel at our best in flannels and look our best, too) and said, thinking Shandean thoughts as he escorted her:

'Ah, yes, you know, but I really couldn't declare him, as you put it, stopped.'

He stood by her, however, not only because he immensely liked her and her husband (their mutual goodness of heart was refreshing, like the staunch sweetness of Francis Allen), but also because she afforded relief from the tensity of feeling induced by dear Dick Fanshawe's religious performance at the wicket. Her motherly presence tempered the strain and the passion of it.

The score stood at sixty-eight. Two maiden overs had been bowled; both bowlers were, in their different way, being drawn into the strained tensity, and one by one, the fieldsmen. Children in arms, sensitive to the atmosphere, began to fret and to cry.

'Sorry, Mr. McLeod, I can't do it,' the hollow voice of Fanshawe sounded out, withstanding the temptation of what old John considered a safe run.

With an exclamation Gauvinier hurriedly pulled out his cigarette case and lighted a cigarette. And no one ventured to throw out cheery encouragement to the batsman: there is a suitability in all things, which men are quick to catch, malign them as cynics may.

Slater (having recovered from the curious superstition that Fanshawe might be tempted to hit) made another frantic effort to york him. The stolidity of his defence suggested that if you could send one down fast enough and suddenly enough you must slip past his guard. Poor Slater nearly twisted his shoulder out of joint in his effort to deliver the ball with the requisite pace and suddenness. But it was no good. It was a fast yorker, right enough, and it beat the batsman right enough but it also beat the wicket-keeper and the dive of short slip, and the grass in its course being unusually short, it reached the boundary just as Fanshawe and old John were starting on their second deliberate run.

Francis inquired of his colleague:

'Was that a bye?'

And his colleague, in anger at the boundary, let loose a surprising volume of shout to the umpire: 'Hit or bye?'

Whereupon the umpire ejaculated 'Hit!' and the wicket-keeper looked as pleased as the bowler looked grieved, and a bitter smile hovered round Fanshawe's lips, it being his first boundary hit of the season. Gauvinier turned his head in the direction in which he knew Oliver was sitting, as though forced to see how the little champion was bearing up, yet not wishing to seem to intrude upon any private passion or sacred grief. He saw the little face stretched and pale with anxiety, his eyes glued upon his adored father's next stroke, and turned away almost abashed, and as though under some unrecognised influence his mind caught the thought like a message from the little boy's intensity: 'Nature meant the old fellow for a hitter.'

Only for a second had his glance been averted from the wicket; it returned to observe the next delivery at which Fanshawe played his stiff, resolute, conscientious, forward shot: but the ball, rising a shade more quickly than others had risen, struck the bat a few inches too high and rose slowly and surely towards Slater, who, moving a few steps forward, brought off an easy catch.

'Oh, he's out, mum!' Paul's quick ear caught a desolate wail, and nothing would have induced him to look at the small champion in his grief. Fanshawe shrugged his shoulders and accepted fate like a Stoic, with grim resignation.

Gauvinier heard: 'There's Polly – look!' and was surprised a moment afterwards to feel himself assaulted, struck on the hip and thigh by what he knew to be the small, and hoped to be the clean, hands of young Oliver Fanshawe.

'A jolly decent innings, Polly,' the little fellow declared with furious defiance. 'You only made a duck; dad's hit a four: a jolly decent innings. He's a jolly fine cricketer and you're a rotten one.'

And he clapped his hands fiercely as his beloved father made his way into the Pavilion. So he worked off on Polly his desire to cry and his unspoken longing that his father should hit a six out of the ground.

72–7–7 read the numbers on the telegraph.

And Oliver rushed back to his mother shouting: 'Cooh! I knew it, seven runs he's made, a four, a two and a one.' And he added, like a man of experience, unconsciously trying to approach the impressive utterance of Sam Bird: 'A jolly useful stand, too, at this stage of the game, I can tell you,' relapsing into a more youthful note to say, chuckling all over:

'Didn't the chaps all jolly well clap him as he came in! Cooh! *My* dad!'

Teddie White was not so much nervous about batting or cricket as about making an exhibition of himself among other men. In consequence the thought of wearing the small blue cap was more painful to him than the thought of making no runs. He had always worn a large cloth cap, except on Sundays, when discomfort was respectable, and his head felt so strange and pinched and airy in the little blue cap large Bannister insisted that he should wear, that he was convinced everyone would notice and deride the strange, pinched airiness of his head. That others wore it without comment was not much consolation; good, sober man that he was, he continued to feel the queerness of his new headpiece. He was a smallish, wiry man with an extremely red face, and he strode quickly out to the wickets holding his bat before him in both hands, a club bat which happened to be a favourite, a good honest weapon which had withstood much hard wear.

Centre, and three more balls to come. The first ball he lashed over cover point's head for four, scattering the tense, religious atmosphere. The second he lifted into the far hedge amid roars of delight from the spectators, who let loose their bottled feelings joyfully, and the third and last he skied high, and mid-off, watching it, watching it, watching it, rise and rise, and drop and drop, held it in spite of the twist put on by the mis-hit; seeing which, White ran back to the Pavilion, shouldering his bat amid laughing acclamations.

Just as when Fanshawe and McLeod were batting, a run seemed almost like a mistake or a profanity, so during this brief display every ball looked like a potential four. Waite remarked to Trine that if the little fellow were coached in proper footwork he would be a really fine hitter. Horace Cairie moaned to Gauvinier: 'If he could only have stayed there for three or four overs!'

Still, eighty was up, and they were within sight almost of the century: oh, if he came off and made a few runs! He felt weak in the stomach and knees as he began to put on his pads. The bowling wasn't so fearfully difficult; the wicket was hard and true. If he could just keep his head and not play the fool at the first few balls: only his legs always shook so much, and it was difficult to hold the bat tightly enough and to watch the ball; when your legs were trembling, there seemed two or three balls coming at you.

He heard Francis call out 80–8–8. For some queer reason the series of eights brought him comfort – his name had been posted for the first XI at the Prep. on the 8th, he had made his top score when he had batted No. 8. He had 8d. in his trouser pocket. He took off his sweater so as to be perfectly ready before large Ted Banninster reached the wicket.

Ted Bannister stood six foot three in his socks, and was broad and stout – a huge man. He loitered genially to the wicket, pleased and confident and proud of the small cap; seeing which Mrs. McLeod, shook with glee, though her face remained sternly controlled. Waite, watching, felt there must be cricket in the man because of his confidence and composure; many in the village felt there must be cricket in him, too. There may have been, but he had never shown visible signs of it. Yet he generally played for Tillingfold because he wanted to play, and he was very large and generally did do what he wanted to do. There was no withstanding his genial, massive insistence. Gauvinier never knew where to put him in the field, for he was slow, very slow, and no catch was he certain of holding. He had dropped some catches so easy that it was almost a feat to drop them. Yet everyone expected that one day he would 'come off' and make a great many runs. He never looked like getting out, yet he invariably did, and promptly.

John was delighted to be batting with his friend. He felt quite certain that Bannister would at last break the run of his bad luck; they would send up the hundred together and place Tillingfold in a safe position. He hit Stevens' first ball for one, and his confidence in Ted Bannister grew while he watched him take centre like a master, removing the bail quietly to make a little mark so that there should be no mistake about his middle and leg – inclining to leg, please.

'Really,' John thought to himself, 'perhaps Mr. Gauvinier ought to put him in earlier. I must mention it to him.'

But this was not to be the day on which Ted Bannister was to show his mettle. For Stevens sent down a slow, straight ball, which gently knocked against his middle stump. John failed to understand why he had not stopped the ball, because he seemed to play at it correctly, a shot which should have returned it nicely back to the bowler, but it didn't; large Ted Bannister retired, pleased and confident and proud of his blue cap, quite unaffected by the little mishap at the wicket.

'This is more like it!' said the excited little scorer to old Francis, and in his excitement called 'Eighty – nine – nought' whereupon old Francis said: 'Steady, mate, I makes it eighty-one.'

'Oh yes, I forgot McLeod's single; eighty-one – nine – nought it is,' he leaned out to shout at the boys who were handling the figures, but Joe Mannerly happened to have taken the job on for a little while, and he, resenting the tone of voice, retorted:

'All right, old cock, I can add one to eighty!'
Which made old Francis chuckle and the Raveley scorer mad.

Horace Cairie only stumbled twice on his way to the wicket. He heard one of the fieldsmen ask the umpire if they would have tea at once or come out to bat for a quarter of an hour, inferring that the innings was already over, and Slater called out to the umpire: 'What is the time, Sam?'

Sam Bird with some difficulty extracted his watch from his tight waistcoat pocket and said, after careful inspection, 'It wants two minutes to the half hour – to half-past fower, that is to say.'

'I could just do with a nice cup o' tea,' someone remarked, and the remark was taken up with variations and passed round the field. Slater, an awfully good fellow, feeling that the insinuation might not be pleasant to the youthful batsman, tried to encourage him by saying that they would probably have some time yet to wait for their tea, the greedy beggars! But the bowler in him could not put conviction into his encouragement. Neither he nor Stevens could have any mercy for the aspirant, however tender his years or however patent was his nervous anxiety to make good. Runs were runs whoever made them, and runs must be prevented.

But the insinuations, though they were depressing, stirred in young Horace that which we may call spunk, and he set his little jaw and gripped his quivering nerves, so that, as he stood facing his first ball from Stevens, his knees hardly trembled at all. And the first ball was a cruel, deadly yorker, likely to prove the undoing of any nervous aspirant, but on it Horace came steady and full, and the firm impact of the bat on the ball turned his confidence from a grain to a regular lump.

Stevens was far too old a hand to get slack in his bowling because it was the last man in and the last man in was a small boy. His next delivery was a perfect length ball on the leg stump, craftily slower, in the confident hope that the little, well-trained schoolboy would play the stock forward shot a little too soon and return a soft catch to the bowler. But Horace, watching the ball like a lynx, without budging his right foot an inch, came forward to it and played it back along the ground like a little book.

Sid Smith from the Pavilion called out loudly and clearly: 'Well played!' and old John McLeod, beaming with approbation, said: 'Oh, good stroke, boy, beautiful, nice stroke!'

Stevens knew from experience that the leg stump was generally the weak spot of young batsmen, who are inclined to edge away from the wicket to avoid the possibility of a bump, so he instinctively bowled to Horace's leg stump. But Horace, though he could never keep his knees from trembling during the first over, was not at all afraid of getting a bump, and hooked the next one (straight at his body but a trifle short) very prettily for two. He was so intent on running that he did not hear the shrill shriek of delight which Oliver Fanshawe let out on seeing his hero, with whom he had spoken that very afternoon, man to man, make a good hit; nearly everyone else on the ground, however, heard it and smiled.

Sid Smith leaned out of the Pavilion and, catching Oliver's eye, called out: 'That's the ticket; you cheer 'im on, mate!'

The poor kid, in his impatience to carry out Sid's instructions, was disappointed that no more runs came that over.

At the end of the over old John McLeod walked across to his colleague at the wicket (the boy was fifteen and the man was fifty, but neither felt the least incongruity in their ages; they were just two sportsmen on equal terms) and said to Horace: 'You're playing beautifully, boy, a lovely, nice game, boy. We must send up the hundred together. Take your own time and think we're batting first, not last. See, boy? First, not last.'

And his arm on Horrie's shoulder pressed it in affection. Then he trotted back to his wicket, happy and beaming; but what would his feelings have been had Gauvinier obeyed Maria's injunctions and declared him stopped? He caught sight of Maria and thought if she had known he would bat all the afternoon, she would not have insisted upon his extra clothing; well as he knew her, he never guessed what she had begged of the captain. If anyone had told him he would not have believed it, knowing her extreme shyness; it is difficult to believe that a person will put her hand in boiling water for your good. Maria, indeed, could not share her husband's delight as much as she would have liked to share it; she was sure that he must be overtiring himself, and terrified that the ball would hit him where he was soft and stout and vulnerable, and do him, perhaps, some serious injury. Her feelings were shared by Horace Cairie's mother, who watched with some anxiety her small son playing this dangerous game among a lot of full-grown men. There was no denying the fact that people had been killed at cricket and damaged for life. Of course, playing with other little boys was different. It seemed only yesterday that Horrie was a baby in arms, and he still liked to sit on her lap sometimes and be petted, 'as though I were a kid again,' as he used to say, the little darling! Still she liked him to be plucky and keen. Only, were those great men being really careful?

Meanwhile, their men-folk at the wicket, the little slim boy and the rubicund stout man, in a very different frame of mind, gradually and steadily, fought for and obtained ascendancy over Slater and Stevens, the bowlers, who, nevertheless, were bowling better than they had bowled at any time throughout the innings. Runs did not come quickly, but they came methodically: a bye and a leg bye; a two to leg from old John: a safe one to cover by Horace, which was turned into three by the rattled fieldsman hurling the ball in recklessly in the vain hope of running out old John, his recklessness presenting Tillingfold and the boy with two runs for the overthrow.

So Slater, seeing that good bowling took no effect except to help the batsmen to play themselves more and more surely in, risked a double change, as bad bowling will sometimes effect what good bowling has failed to accomplish. He replaced Stevens by a long young gentleman who kept racehorses, and whose idea of bowling was to despatch the ball somehow with all his might at the wicket; it would not be accurate to call him erratic because the word implies some basis of intention from which the bowler often wanders. Pethering had no standard of intention except, perhaps, to smash the stumps.

He took a longish run, which he ended with a jump, sometimes well over the crease, as Sam Bird knew, and in consequence kept a careful eye open for no-balls. His action was so surprising that a few people shared his own illusion that he was a good bowler. He sometimes smashed a wicket down in his first over, which Slater hoped would be the case now. Slater never kept him on for more than three overs, and in consequence Pethering considered himself unjustly treated, as he despised the bowling of Slater and Stevens. So he rushed and jumped and hurled the ball towards Horace, a full pitch, hip high, which Horace, unbudging as a little rock, met with his bat and put to the long leg boundary. The next ball was a bumping long hop, which Horace made no attempt to touch. The third ball was a really good one, which beat Horace completely and missed his bails by three or four inches, whereupon Pethering held his head in his hands and stamped with disappointment.

Sid Smith thought his expression of disappointment overdone, so he called out in a cheery, loud voice:

'You'll get him next time – perraps,' and the last word filled the cheery comment with derisive meaning which was keenly appreciated by many in the field and all in the Pavilion.

A yell of joy went up when the boy hooked a short one at his body fearlessly for two, and Waite remarked that the little chap was a born cricketer. His mother began to fear that young Oliver Fanshawe would upset himself with excitement, for he danced and capered and swung his arms and shrieked with shrill ecstasy at every shot of his hero. Gauvinier strode about, a great smile on his face, beside himself with delight, saying: 'Isn't he a little ripper?' to everyone he met: but the batsmen's womenfolk, Maria and Horrie's mother, became more and more restless and anxious; they, at any rate, shared Pethering's own notion that he was a terrible bowler.

Two more runs off a lucky snick to leg and ninety-eight was reached. Oh, if only he could send up the century with the last balls of the over! The wild hope unsettled him, and he mistimed the shortish ball on his body and the ball hit him high up on the thigh and he overbalanced and fell.

The silly mid-on was rubbing him before he had hardly time to get up; fieldsmen clustered round him, hoping he wasn't hurt. Horace repeated:

'It's all right, thanks, absolutely all right,' anxious to get on with his innings, terrified lest his mater might come out on the pitch and make a fuss. His quick eye caught a glimpse of her, risen and hesitating.

'You wait a bit. Take your time. Give it a good rub,' the kindly fieldsmen grouped round urged him, but Horace protested desperately, seeing his mater begin to move.

'Oh, come on! Come on! I'm *all right*,' and hobbled to the wicket, just in time to prevent his mother's further approach.

He got a tremendous cheer, which he didn't much like, as he felt he had been making a song about nothing.

It was old John's privilege to send up the century, which he did with a beautiful cut for four, his best shot in the match.

Horace did his best to run the bye which followed with as little limp as possible, hating to show off in any way, but the bang made his leg ache.

Whether it was due to his leg or to over-excitement, or to relaxation on passing the century can never be known, but the next ball he played hard on to his foot, and it rolled back, hit the wicket, and the leg bail dropped off. So his foot was sore now as well as his hip, but his heart was light and gay and happy (after the sharp pang of getting out) because he had done what he so tremendously wanted to do.

Cheers and shouts greeted the retiring batsmen, in which all the Raveley fieldsmen joined. Everyone's heart felt warm to the little slim sportsman and the oldish stout rubicund sportsman, and both sportsmen were as happy as man or boy can be: happy with a solid, shy, quivering happiness.

'One hundred and three – ten – thirteen,' called out old Francis, glowing with pleasure at his small friend's success. The last wicket had put on twenty-two runs. Old John McLeod, carrying his bat right through the innings, had made twenty-three not out.

Horace, having taken his pads off, his back sore with congratulatory slaps, was obliged to go up to his mother – not that she in the least understood what he had done, but because he wanted to be near her in his intense happiness. He came towards her red and bright-eyed, limping now perhaps the merest shade more than was quite necessary (from her he loved quiet sympathy, and it was beastly sore, really). As he came she remembered him, an even smaller boy, praying at her knee: 'Oh, God, please bless mum and dad, and keep me safe through the night, and oh, God, *please* make me a sportsman!' and wondered if perhaps the prayer had been answered.

She asked him why he had hit the ball on to his foot and then on to the wicket, and he answered, proud of his mater, loving her to tease him, and talk to him like that and not sort of smarm over him like some chaps' maters did:

'Oh, because I was an utter juggins!'

And he thought that she looked simply ripping.

'I say,' he said, feeling gloriously a man, 'I'll get tea sent out to you as soon as ever I can.'

But she told him that he need not bother, as she was taking tea with a friend in the village.

He escorted her a little way across the field, then ran back to take tea in the Pavilion.

Cheers and shouts greeted the retiring batsmen.

Chapter Six

THE TEA INTERVAL

At a Committee Meeting of the Tillingfold Cricket Club, held in the Village Reading Room at the beginning of the season, an ex-captain of the club had proposed that the tea interval should be abolished, or, if not abolished, at any rate greatly curtailed. Why waste time at tea and let the interest of the game flag by a succession of intervals? Were cricketers a lot of old women to need tea? In his young days players never thought of taking tea. Tea – each time he brought the word out he pronounced it with more biting scorn. He had often ridden on his bicycle five miles without his dinner to a game of cricket and had taken neither bite nor sup till he had bicycled five miles home again after the game; and now the game had hardly begun when all the players trooped off the field to tea –

The Committee listened in respectful, horror-stricken silence. It was the sort of uncomfortable proposal which Dick Fanshawe was forced by his nature to support, and he lugubriously supported it. It struck so deep that all were too dismayed to oppose it. The Chairman had not the heart to put the motion before the meeting, thus numb and dumb with dismay. There was a fidgeting, uneasy and prolonged silence, which was immensely enjoyed by Francis Allen, who knew very well that whether the players took tea or not, his wife would always bring down his tea, and a very nice tea, to the scoring-box. At last, however, he came to the rescue and suggested that perhaps visiting teams might miss their tea; and it might seem funny not to have tea at Tillingfold when they had tea wherever they visited. Whereupon Gauvinier, speaking merely as captain, begged to point out that he would not like to be responsible for the fielding or batting either of his friend Mr. Fanshawe or of his friend, the ex-captain, if they tried to perform in either capacity without a proper tea: he did not wish to be personal, but he had noticed that the two men who partook more heartily than any others of tea were precisely his worthy friends, the ex-captain and Mr. Fanshawe.

The spirits of the Committee rose from cold dismay to loud, glad laughter, and the motion was never put to the meeting.

It may be a matter for dispute whether a tea interval is necessary in a first-class three-day match, which we mostly visit as eager spectators well equipped with acid drops and sandwiches, with pleasant booths and bars within easy reach, but in a half-day village cricket match the tea interval is an outstanding feature of the match.

Drawn games are rare, when the weather holds. The necessity for making runs quickly causes every batsman to take risks; the whole spirit of the game differs entirely from the leisurely, business-like excellence of a first-class three-day match: the difference is that between a ten-mile walking race and a hundred yards sprint. The cricket is not so good; the game is infinitely better, except, perhaps, in the decisive testmatch of the rubber.

Tea was taken in the Pavilion. Two long tables set together with long wooden forms on either side and forms by the edge of the Pavilion under the open shutters.

Plates piled with cut bread and butter, paste sandwiches, sometimes cucumber sandwiches, sometimes plates of lettuce; small plates of cakes which were replenished, a hint, perhaps, from the caterer that the excellent game of eating a good nine-pennyworth in ten minutes could perhaps be too easily won if an unscrupulous direct attack were made upon the cakes. At the top of the table stood an enormous urn of boiling water, three large teapots and a goodly array of plain white cups. You helped yourself to milk and sugar.

Slowly the men crowded in through the swing door from the changing room – players, scorers, umpires and a few supporters of the visiting team.

Always there was a general pause of silence and good manners, a queer constraint at sight of the food and seats, which lasted until places were gradually taken and a cup of tea or a slice of bread and butter handled. The first few cups of tea and plates of bread and butter were stiffly handled, and in a few minutes everyone was comfortably helping himself and passing it on and chatting and laughing.

There were flowers on the table to-day; marguerite daisies and maiden-hair fern; there were cucumber sandwiches and lettuces and a plate of radishes. The white tables looked pretty and inviting. Even the slight smell of oil and the Pavilion (a peculiar smell which you got to like after playing a few seasons for Tillingfold) was friendly and pleasant; and the green ground in the hot sun outside and the distant hedges and trees on to the village and the hills looked gay and fresh and beautiful.

Gauvinier wished that he had made a few runs so that he could have needed tea, but even though he had made none, he didn't do badly, and he always enjoyed being in the crowded Pavilion thick with men at their good-natured best for a little while.

'Well, I dunno. Might p'raps sit down.'
'Not a bad notion.'
'Middlin' warm out there.'
'Cup o' tea?'
'Ah, shouldn't mind!'
'After you.'
'Go on.'
'Well, thanks very much.'
'Two – yes – if you don't mind. And a drop of milk.'
'That's more like it.'
'A cupper tea (sips) refreshing. Not 'alf.' (Sucks moustache.)
'Middlin' warm out there.' (Sips, sips, sips.)
'Nine-pence, I b'lieve.'
'That's good; known it a bob some places.'
'Ah, and fifteen-pence.'
'Robbery, that is.'
'Everyone for theirselves.'
'You're right, no mistake.'
'There's old Teddie White with his face as long as a June day.'
'Ah! His winner ain't come home. Sure snip, too.'
'Mug's game backin' 'orses.'
'Don't mind if I do. Thanks.'
'Not too bad, this paste.'
'Nor ain't the cu-cumber.'
'If I ate a bit of that now I'd taste it the rest of the evening, I would, straight.'
'I fancies a bit of cu-cumber wonnerful with me tea. Sundays or anything like that. If there's a cu-cumber anywhere about, my missus is sure to get hold of him.'
'A nice stick of celery now.'
'Ah! after a touch o' frost.'
'Wonnerful wholesome stuff celery, they say.'
'And I'm one for a raw onion and bit o' cheese with a glass o' beer. *You* know – for your supper, like.'

Teddie White had never seen a horse race, and had never ridden a horse, but he backed the horses he had never seen with assiduity and kept a small book of their form and the weights they carried. To hear him talk of horses you would have thought that he had spent his life among them; but his knowledge was at second or third hand. A charm was lent to his betting transactions by their being surreptitious and mysterious. He felt that he was 'in the know.' Only with favoured friends did he expand at all on the subject.

His face now was black and gloomy. He had backed a winner; and the kindly 'bus driver who put his half-crowns on for him had just returned his half-crown (or another) saying he was sorry that he had been prevented from seeing the bookmaker. Horrid doubts raged in poor Teddie's mind, for *Shake-your-Heels* had won at 10 to 1. He felt that he had been robbed of ten half-crowns, which (his arithmetic affected by his fury) he worked out at forty-five shillings.

The tea tasted filthy; the bread and butter was sand in his mouth. He stood in morose loneliness on the edge of the throng and it looked as though his family would not have a comfortable week-end, unless, somehow, the bile he was storing within him was released. Not even the acclamations which greeted old John's triumphant entry could pierce his distress and touch him, though old John McLeod and he were on friendly terms.

Waite deftly taking tea, standing by Edgar Trine, standing also, caught some of that young gentleman's extreme good-nature and went straight up to old John, making his way through the crowd, for he felt that old John had avoided his eye uneasily and wished no cloud to dull the old fellow's triumph.

Waite put his hand on John's shoulder (so perfect were his manners that the tea-cup affected him as little as it would have affected a waiter or a curate) and said: 'A real good innings, sir; good, sound batting. Our little misfortune would never have happened if we had come to an understanding, as I am sure we should very soon do.'

'All my silly fault! All my silly fault!' spluttered old John happily, his mouth full of bread and butter, and he took a hearty sip of tea to help the process of mastication, hoping Waite would not stand long behind his back, 'I'm most all-firedly sorry about it.'

'Don't you believe him, sir,' said Bannister. 'He ran you out o' set purpose, knowing he'd never have the breath to carry his bat if you stopped in too long.'

'He's an artful one, our Secretary,' Sid Smith called out, and he turned to Stevens, the imperturbable bowler, whom he always delighted to chaff.

'Can't bowl against boys, Jim, can you, mate? Not cunning and crool enough to knock a nipper's wicket down. You just played your eye in proper on old Jim here, didn't you, Horrie? Ah, but he can bowl, you know, when he puts his mind to it; but he likes to see the last man setting the runs up, just when he thinks he'll slip into the Pavilion for a nice cup of tea. It was warm out there, Jim, warn't it, mate?'

'Middlin' hot, Sid, you're right. The nipper can bat.'

The 'nipper' was so excited that he leaned across the table to call out at Sid:

'I was bucked to make a few, because all the fellows began to talk about tea when I came out as though it were all over, and it just wasn't quite.'

Sid beamed at the boy's bubbling keenness, then grew solemn to announce:

'Ah! you trust Raveley to think about tea, all right. Some chaps likes cricket – ' he left a gap, filled by an expressive nod, for what other chaps liked. There was a general laugh, and shouts of protest, among which the voice of the eager little wicket-keeper could be heard asking Sid Smith when he went without his tea last. It came from between a munch and a sip: cup in one hand, slice of bread and butter in the other, and was polished off with a gulp of tea on the munch.

Sid Smith eyed him blandly and retorted: 'Ah! I get what I can while I can, mate, when you're about.'

At which a roar of laughter broke upon the little wicket-keeper, who was obviously eager at his tea as at the wicket. But he, not easily embarrassed, stuffed the finish of his slice into his grinning mouth and reached out for a cake, a doughnut, which he did not wish to lose.

'I always fancies the Tillingfold teas,' he confided to his neighbour.

Two reasons combined to move John McLeod from his seat, which he rarely abandoned until the very end of tea. The proximity of Waite caused him uneasiness, although, having no eyes in his back, he could not see that perfect gentleman, who was conversing with Sam Bird, with the ease with which he conversed with ladies at Beckenham, and he noticed gloom on the features of Teddie White which caused a vague 'Shall I?' to become a definite 'I will' in his kindly, impulsive mind. So with some difficulty he shifted himself out from the table and, praying that he might neither upset his tea-cup nor drop his bread and butter, made his way to Teddie White.

Now, to carry his bat through an innings had long been his cherished wish, and he was anxious to celebrate the day on which his wish had at last been fulfilled, as a great occasion. This could be done by asking a few friends in to supper, the Bannisters, namely, and the Whites, and old Francis, perhaps, and his wife, if he could get them. They would have a song or two and a little something nice to eat and to drink – *you* know, a jolly sort of evening. Time to get home and have a bit of a wash – say a half after eight. Goodness! he'd like to have asked the whole team – ah, and the Raveley chaps too – to a swank sit-down supper at 'The Dog and Duck.'

He explained this all to Teddie White, who never greeted an invitation of any kind with enthusiasm, though he had, after much cajoling, passed many a pleasant evening with the McLeods. His gloom instantly deepened. It was rather a funny thing to change your plans for an evening so sudden. He doubted his wife might not have got her shopping in, and the girl (his daughter) would be wanting her supper. He was interrupted. What did he think? Why, of course the girl must come too. My goodness, yes, when she was one of the prettiest girls in Tillingfold. Ah, that was all very well, but who knew when she would be in? Why, leave a note and she'd pop round when she did come in: and bring her boy, too, if there was one. That, too, was all very well, but Teddie White himself didn't know as he felt quite in the mood like, not to-night, for a party. Oh, yes, he did; it would take his mind off his bit of bad luck, of which John had already heard; and cursed again in his heart Teddie's love of backing horses, which kept his otherwise sober friend from some nice hobby and got on his nerves and put temptation in everybody's way, making illwill and bad feeling and the wrong sort of excitement, which turned decent interest as flat as stale ale.

At length Teddie White owned that he would be glad to come. He always enjoyed John's hospitality so much that he was anxious not to appear in any way to jump at an invitation which he considered should be accepted with a becoming reluctance. And John hastened away to get his teacup replenished and to invite the other Ted – Ted Bannister – who declared himself delighted without any hesitation at all, for Bannister had, among other accomplishments, a fine bass voice which he thought even finer than it was, and was accustomed to be the life and soul of many gatherings, smoking concerts and others. The sight of him made many small boys begin to hum:

> So sit yourself on the sofa, Sam,
> And make yourself at home,
> What do I care
> Whether you air
> From Africa or Rome –

which began the chorus of one of his most popular comic songs, which related the sad experiences of an amorous darkie. He sang with the same full-blooded unconcern to niddling detail (such as the right note) with which he played cricket, and no little *contretemps* (such as getting out) upset his composure.

Sid Smith caught Gauvinier's eye.

'That's a nice little pond you've got at your place,' he said, with such innocence that Gauvinier answered quite seriously:

'Yes, it is jolly; we want to get some water-lilies to grow in it.'

Just right to hatch some nice birds out on.'

'Oh, not large enough!'

'Not large enough for one nice duck's egg?'

There was a burst of laughter.

'Sid, you devil, you fairly had me that time,' said Gauvinier, laughing at the ancient wheeze.

'Don't you break him in your pocket as you takes him home. Have him boiled for your supper even if you don't hatch him out.'

'He ought to have him poached on toast.'

'I'll wait for that till next Saturday; have two then, my boy, with a one before 'em.'

'Oh, that's the ticket. And you might get one more, too, just as nice and simple as you got him to-day.'

'Oh, don't say that, Sid, I'd rather take a hundred.'

'I'd like to see you get it, too. I would that.'

Sam Bird disliked hurry and disliked waste of time; both he avoided with quiet care, especially during the tea interval, for Gauvinier was apt to keep a sharp eye on the time, and required Sam, quite properly, to lead the way into the field again. Sam was not in the least disconcerted by Waite's efforts at conversation. He attended steadily to the business in hand, and never allowed speech or any other frivolity to distract his attention from it. He had long ago acquired proficiency in the knack of chewing and speaking at the same time. The caterer's little wife wore a harassed look on her face whenever she caught sight of his impenetrable calm, to which cakes and bread and butter were drawn as by a charm, to disappear, alas! to disappear. Waite squeezed himself by Bird, to discuss the position of the game.

'Are we safe?' he asked.

Sam slowly turned, munching, crushing rather, half a rock cake to pulp in his mouth:

'We should be, Mr. Waite, but cricket . . . cricket is a hazardous game, sir, and we can never know for certain. Still, if all goes well . . . if all goes well . . . I should say as we were . . . middlin' safe.'

'What sort of bowling have we got?'

'On their day, Mr. Waite . . . on their day, both our worthy captain and Sid Smith there can put down . . . can put down a very good ball. Tom Hunter – in that far corner, there – Tom Hunter is not too bad as a change. After that, Mr. Waite . . . after that we're a little weak, sir, a little weak, I fear. I was most distressed to see a batsman like you run out. Most foolish piece of work.'

'Oh, the best men lose their heads at times.'

'Most foolish piece of work, sir, most foolish and unfortunate. You don't – er – you don't trundle the leather yourself, sir, I presume?'

'Oh, no, no! Not even seventh change,' said Waite, with a touch (*dictu mirabile*) of bashfulness.

One hundred and three – one hundred and three – the numbers kept beating through Horace Cairie's mind. It wasn't very much, a hundred and three, if once runs began to come.

'Are you fearfully strong in batting?' he ventured to ask Jim Stevens, who was sitting near him.

'Not too bad,' replied the imperturbable Jim. 'Some and some.'

'What's your highest score this year?'

'One hundred and forty-eight 'gainst Purmingstowe.'

'Nothing to what you'd do against Smock Alley or Roundabout,' called out Sid, referring to two tiny hamlets in the neighbourhood, a bundle of cottages merely.

'You eat your tea, mate, quietly; you'll need all you can put away before we've done with you.'

'It'll be just right now for fielding, out there. You ought to teach that captain of yours to win the toss like I've taught ours. And he needed some teaching. But you can do anything with kindness. What sort of a ball was that you bowled poor Tommie Hunter with, eh? Some fellers 'ud do anything. Wouldn't they, Tom? Never mind, we'll get a little of our own back soon. Wait till old Tom there sets about 'em. He'll show you how to bowl a nice full toss, won't you, Tom?'

'Well, don't put him too high,' laughed Slater. 'And I'll show you how to put him away. But as a matter of fact, that one slipped out of my fingers.'

'We knew he was a fluke right enough,' said Sid, and Tom asserted not crossly now, but with a large, shy smile on his large, round face:

'I could 'ave swore he was well above my head.'

'And the bail went twenty-seven yards,' called out the eager little wicket-keeper. 'Jolly glad he didn't get into my eyeball. I've known a feller have his eye cut clean out by a bail. Leastways, I've read of it.'

'Twenty-eight yards it were,' announced Stevens.

'That's eighty-four feet,' said Fanshawe.

'As good at sums as he is at hitting fours,' commented Sid.

'All right, Sid,' said Dick, who was meant to hear the comment. 'At any rate, I wouldn't go trying to smash a man's hands out of spite because I funked his bowling. Some of us were brought up to think of others.'

'And how often do you suppose I've told him to keep those great hairy hands of his where they're wanted? Nets, I call 'em. Serve 'em right if they did get broke.'

'I lay that ball was travelling,' said old Francis. 'As nice a catch that as ever I did see.'

'Go on, now! Don't make the feller conceited.'

And Horace Cairie wondered how Sid Smith could rag so unconcernedly when such a lot depended on his bowling, and a hundred and three was really not a very good score on such a wicket: with the ground so fast that almost any hit might be a four. And time was getting on surely; yet Sam Bird proceeded with his tea as though he had only just begun, and everyone began to loll back with cigarettes as though they were going to sit and smoke all the rest of the afternoon: and Dick Fanshawe was slowly lighting a pipe. Half-past five – six: half-past six – seven: oh, in an hour or two they would all know who had won the game.

John slipped out as was his custom to have a word with Maria and tell her that it would be all right, he had spoken to Jennings (the caterer); she could slip into the Pavilion when the players had finished and have a nice cup of tea.

'Well, I had a cup, dear, before I left home, and a biscuit, to make sure,' Maria

replied, as she invariably replied, and thanked John for his forethought. A chat with Mrs. Jennings and another tea helped to pass the time, which, she would have been burned alive before she confessed, hung a little heavy at cricket matches, sitting hour after hour, hoping that that hard ball was not going to strike against any round soft place on her dear husband's body.

'You must be wore out already, John, running about out there holdin' that bat and wearin' them great pads. I tremble to think what a state you'll be in by the end of the evening.'

'Maria, my love, it's a great occasion this. Don't you understand I've carried my bat all through the innings? Went in first and never got out. I've always wished to do that, all my life, Maria.'

'I'm glad you've got your wish, dear. I'm sure you ought to get all your wishes, they're that kind and good: but why you should wish to run about at your age all the afternoon out there in the hot sun, I don't know.'

John always pretended not to hear what he did not want to hear, so he went on, quite unabashed:

'As it's a great occasion, my love, I've asked the Bannisters and the Whites to come in for a jolly sort of evening, *you* know.'

'That will be nice,' said the good Maria, who never found anything a trouble which could please John. 'I'll just slip back into the village before the shops get too crowded and get in one or two things. It's wonderful what you can get nowadays all ready for eating.'

John leaned over her to whisper: 'If I'd known I was going to carry my bat I'd never have wore that little undervest.'

'Don't say such a thing now, John! Won't you need it, standing out there with the evening drawing on!'

'I'm that perr-spiring hot, Maria . . .' he leaned forward to whisper suddenly: 'A nice claret cup, eh! For a treat! What do you say? Get some ice at Daubers if you can. A lemon or two; two or three bottles of that Australian Burgundy, half a dozen syphons. We'll have the big glasses, too, Maria . . . oooh! I could do with one now – no mistake.'

'Do mind you don't get overdoing it, running about out there, John. I'm quite used to you in your little cap, dear,' she added. 'It suits you lovely. I think all of you look very smart in them.'

'More of a team like, altogether.'

'Yes, exactly; much more like a team, to be sure. Most suitable, and I do hope it's a proper protection against the sun, dear.'

'Fine! Couldn't be better. But I must be getting along, Maria, my dear.'

Meanwhile, in the Pavilion Gauvinier was beginning to grow restive as Sam Bird, despite several hints of gesture with his thumb towards the deserted wickets, seemed to become more and more solidly established in his seat, as though soon he must take root and grow there; and showed no sign whatever of ceasing the slow persistence with which he continuously ate. He liked one or two to lead the way always, and himself to sit where he was sitting. There was only one other umpire, and Sam never liked to make his way with only one other man to the wicket. Yet umpires must lead the way. Sam carried his natural diffidence too far. Some minutes had passed since the church clock struck the quarter. Time was valuable.

'Well, we'd better be going. I suppose,' Gauvinier announced in a loud and cheery voice, well aware that '*Sussex won't be druv*,' and wondering, as he always wondered, wherever he should place Ted Bannister in the field.

'Get your pads on, Jim,' he said to Saddler, who was always ready to start, and had put them on before tea so as not to be hurried.

This pleased Saddler, and helped to rub in the suggestion that it was time to get out into the field.

Sid Smith got up and stretched.

'Oh, curse it,' muttered Gauvinier to himself, hurrying across to Slater, for he had forgotten to ask him to get someone to collect the nimble ninepences from his team and to get anyone to collect from his own. Ted Bannister was just the man for the job, and he was always obliging enough to consent at once, as Gauvinier himself detested handling money and giving change, and natural diffidence kept others from liking that or any other work which entailed the least semblance of responsibility or 'pushing oneself forward.' Yet the caterer preferred that a member of the team should collect rather than that each man should pay as he left. He feared forgetfulness, especially, odd as it may seem, from such gentry as might be playing, as they were accustomed, perhaps, to find tea ready for them without asking questions as to how it got there, wherever they might be. In the same way they supposed, often enough, that cups and saucers washed themselves up.

Slater and Ted Bannister collected the money, promptly, with the usual jokes about change and how much each got out of the handed hat. The dressing-room became a scramble of men removing jackets and sweaters, tightening up belts and scarves, then emptied slowly round the Pavilion, where they stood shyly, hands in pockets, waiting, keen, expectant, yet anxious to appear, for some good British reason, nonchalant and at perfect ease, which only Waite and Trine actually achieved, the one result, no doubt, of their expensive education.

At last they made a move, Tom Hunter hugging his arms and walking gingerly; Trine eager for the ball, which Sam, a little ahead, jerked at him; Sid Smith chewing a bent; John McLeod fidgeting with his cap and feeling very pleased with himself; Waite talking to Teddie White, who happened to be next him; Horace Cairie hoping that he would not be put to field at *leg*, which he considered dull, and longing for *mid-on*, where hot ones came; Dick Fanshawe trying to wipe from his mind the horrid vision of a slow, high, easy catch coming straight towards him; Ted Bannister confident that in his cap and white shoes he was a fine figure of a cricketer; Gauvinier beginning to tingle all over with the desire to get the team as one man together for the dismissal of the Raveley men, and feeling a curious and delightful kinship with old John and young Horace and Sid Smith and Jim Saddler that flickered out towards White and Waite and Trine and drew in Tom Hunter, and only quailed before the large expansive Bannister, who seemed to have no cricket in him that Gauvinier ever could find. And underneath this curious sense of kinship glowed a deeper, more constant feeling, that took its life from other matters than a game – the feeling of friendship for Dick Fanshawe.

'Mid-off, Dick.'

'Right-o,' came the rather sad response.

'Point, John.'

'Fancy putting a boy like that at point,' commented Sid, and old John warned him with a 'Now then, Sid,' pitching the ball he had just received at his head, which Sid caught and jerked trickily at Horace, pretending a fast one and sending a very slow one which the boy, stumbling laughing forward, after his first step back, missed.

'Mid-on, Horrie.'

'Oh, good!'

'Do you mind taking leg, Mr. Bannister? We always want a good man there to stop whacks off Sid's full tosses.'

'Anywhere you like, sir.'

'If only he were as good a fieldsman as he is a genial fellow,' thought Gauvinier, and chid himself for injustice. That was one of the unpardonable things about Bannister: he always made you feel unjust.

'Sid starts at the far end.'

'Cover, Waite?'

'You're sure you've no one else . . .'

'No, no! cover.'

'Trine, deep. A bit on the leg. Teddie, deep mid-wicket. Sid'll put you where he wants you. Tom, third man, not too deep, you know, and bowl this end.'

Three or four men came up and asked which end began. He told them. The fieldsmen who might possibly be affected by the sun, looked at it and shaded their eyes, hoping that spectators and others would thereby realise the extreme difficulty of bringing off any catch that might come their way. The sun covers a multitude of sins, for few realise how rarely a ball comes in the direct line of the sun compared with how often the fieldsman dazzles himself by looking quite unnecessarily full into the sun.

Chapter Seven

TILLINGFOLD FIELD

As a member of the Selection Committee Gauvinier had steadily insisted upon one point for many years: that as in their team there was no man who could be relied upon to make runs, keenness in the field must influence selection more than anything else. In his early days as captain, his outspoken attacks on slack fielding had made such a stir that a special committee had been called at which the chairman had voiced a formal complaint; the men would not really stand being shouted at in public like a lot of schoolboys; they'd had enough of the sergeant-major. They considered they knew their places in the field without being shifted about so much. Cricket was, after all, a game, and though keenness was excellent, it could be overdone, and if he might venture upon personal criticism, at which he did hope Mr. Gauvinier would not take offence, he should say that his fault (we all have faults, haven't we?) was that he was over-anxious – over-anxious, you understand? a little over-anxious.

Gauvinier had apologised for any hastiness in his make-up; had pointed out that if he were more than they could stand, they had only to elect another captain, and delivered a homily upon the importance of keen fielding, stating that slackness in the field sickened his soul and would always sicken it; that he feared that he would never be able to hide his feelings; that they had better not be too sensitive and had better say out to him what they felt, man to man, than go grousing about among themselves. His words aroused the strange blend of liking and loathing which his conduct was apt to provoke, and the meeting ended in an unanimous vote of confidence in him as captain.

So it came about that keenness in the field was the fashion in Tillingfold cricket. Small boys jeered loose fielding and hooted mistakes in the field. Cigarettes were never smoked except furtively in a second knock. Aspirants to the team practised fielding, and Gauvinier kept his mouth shut as closely as possible while the visiting side batted. He withstood the temptation of telling a fieldsman who had stepped nimbly from a fast one that it was the wrong time to be thinking of his wife and family.

Visiting teams used often to comment: 'Pretty smart in the field,' 'Mis-sed catches lost matches,' and the subject would run pleasantly on to the true conclusion that good fielding won more games, really, than anything else. Bowling or batting lay too much on the lap of the gods: well, any young chaps could learn how to field. You might or might not make runs or get wickets, but, hang it! you could be on your toes in the field, whoever you were.

But could Ted Bannister? could Ted Bannister? Gauvinier wondered in dismay.

The imperturbable Stevens was making his slow way to the wicket, accompanied by the eager little wicket-keeper, Joe Stonor, who seemed to be trotting by his side very much as a small terrier trots by a large Newfoundland. They were Raveley's well-known first pair, and at sight of them Gauvinier was tempted to call in Trine and Waite from the deep, and would have done so had he not known that a change in the customary placing of his field would have caused Sid to bowl half volleys and full tosses which even those stickers might have a go at. And anyhow, their careful range of strokes was well covered by the field as it was placed.

'It's one thing to bowl all through an innings, Jim,' said Sid. 'It's another thing to bat all through.'

'It depends who's bowling at you,' remarked Stevens.

'Of course you *would* make the poor little feller take first ball.'

''Twas his wish,' answered Stevens, slowly, smiling.

'We know all about that!' said Sid, impressively, somehow managing to infer that the poor little fellow had been bullied into it; and Horrie, at mid-on, thought:

'Yes; he does rag too much,' in dismay, for the best people at his small school never engaged in any preliminary banter with their opponents, and he wanted his hero, Sid, to be perfect in every particular. He never excused Sid to himself by thinking: 'Oh, well, this is only village cricket.' Such a thought would have seemed blasphemous to his passionate love of Tillingfold and the game; also he had experienced both as spectator and player a keenness quite as great in village matches as any he had yet played at school. And, after all, there was something rather splendid in Sid's ease and confidence, which perhaps, when he was Sid's age, he himself would be able to feel.

He loved fielding mid-on, because that was the place where batsmen tried to steal runs and, if you kept on your toes, you could rattle 'em up a bit if they tried to take any liberties, and you might, too, have some smart drives to stop and, perhaps, with luck, a smart catch to hold. He felt it an honoured position and determined to rise to the occasion. Every ball he would watch on to the bat and off it.

Ted Bannister adjusted his cap and stood with his arms folded, the picture of leisurely, large good-nature. Gauvinier eyeing him wickedly wished for a long, invisible pin. And Tom Hunter, the grouser at the moment in ascendancy over the sportsman, wondered why the deuce he had not been put on to bowl at Sid's end, which, he felt convinced, would suit him far better than the end at which he was bowling. He held his elbows in either hand and stepped from one foot to another.

'A little squarer and closer, Tom,' Gauvinier said to him. 'For little flicks, you know, not cuts. We shan't have many of them.'

Tom grinned and shuffled quickly into the right place; but he thought horrid thoughts about Gauvinier's bossiness and fussiness and what a mucking shame it was to have a Gentlemen's Cricket Club. He hadn't quite warmed up to it yet.

The Raveley umpire, his block having been given to the eager little wicket-keeper, called 'Play,' and the word sent a little shock through every fieldsman except Ted Bannister, who maintained his leisurely, benevolent stance. Jim Saddler buckled himself up behind the wicket, watching Sid's arm as intently as the eager little batsman. Sid took three easy steps towards the crease and, swinging his arm rather low, delivered the ball with the ease of action of a born bowler. Medium to slow, the books would call him. On his day he could vary the pace and flight of the ball so well that the best batsman might be deceived. He could break in, too, from the off rather more than you would expect. His first ball was a fast yorker; his second a slowish yorker, and on both of them Joe came down with all his little weight, plomp and fierce, like a cat on a mouse trying to run under her. The third was short and fast and widish on the off, and Jim Saddler was thankful to feel it smack nicely into his right hand, as Joe Stonor had never moved his bat towards it, fearful of being caught. Old John began to get excited because it would be off just such a ball that some batsman would send him a sharp catch. Ah! Goodness! How he hoped it would stick in his hand! Waite at cover thought to himself that he would mostly get mis-hits off half volleys if such balls were often let alone. Such a ball to him would have meant four at any period of his innings.

Trine picked a small buttercup in the deep and gave up any fond hopes of a decent catch yet awhile.

A good-length ball on his legs, Joe stepped injudiciously away from his wicket to play, and missed; Jim Saddler missed it too, as Gauvinier thought he might, who, jumping from short slip, stopped it, to Jim's delight, with his left hand.

'Well fielded!' called out Sid, and Waite felt pleased to be playing under an alert captain.

'You've got a reach!' remarked Tom Hunter, grinning, as Gauvinier resumed his place, the sportsman in him for a moment emerging to almost level terms with the grouser.

'Sid's in form to-day,' Gauvinier said, stepping into position. 'I can smell it. You see if I'm not right.'

And Tom Hunter, also stooping forward, wondered why the hell it was necessary for anyone to have favourites. 'Rotten captain!' he thought, the sportsman in him subsiding. Bad thoughts clouded his mind, and when Joe struck sharply at a good-length ball on the off from Sid, and misjudging its flight sent Tom a quick, low catch, he, through lack of attention, was flurried, over-balanced in that all-important fraction of a second, and though the ball hit his hand and was stopped, the catch, which he would under other circumstances have held (as he was a clever fieldsman), was, alas! dropped.

'Oh! well tried, Tom!' cried Gauvinier and some others; but Tom, knowing his own powers, was riled and humiliated.

'Sorry, Sid!' he called out with real sincerity in his voice as he returned the ball to the bowler, whose feelings were very mixed, what with keen sympathy for his friend Tom in missing a catch, and what with annoyance at missing a good wicket, for eager little Joe could be troublesome, and Tom was considered a safe catch; indeed he was one of the best fieldsmen on the side.

'Anyone might have missed that!' said Gauvinier. His spurt of fury at a dropped catch having passed, he was anxious that Tom should not feel depressed.

'Ah!' confessed Tom, with that touch of honesty which made Gauvinier like him awfully, 'I was thinking of other things.' There was nothing to be said in answer, but the man in both felt recognition for an instant and both were greatly cheered – heartened as a drink heartens a thirsty man.

'Jolly glad he didn't come to me,' said old John, beaming. 'Jolly glad. Couldn't have stooped to touch him, not *touch* him.' Which was probably quite true.

Horrie was in dismay. He thought of the horrible saying: 'Dropped Catches Lost Matches,' and remembered that dropping catches was said to be as infectious as the measles. Fortunately the next ball was hit in his direction, and he flew at it with such vigour that the batsmen thought it wiser, after two or three shouts, not to attempt the run on which they had started.

In crossing for the over Horrie was delighted to hear Gauvinier say quietly, in tones of warm approval: 'Good boy; they won't steal many runs from you.'

Tom Hunter took a jerky little run with skips in it, and delivered the ball very high, bending his head forward in a way which reminded some people of an old cat washing behind his ears. He endeavoured to bowl a little faster always than he could quite manage, and from time to time delivered a slow ball, which even the jerks and skips in his run proclaimed was coming. This ball, however, was occasionally successful, not so much because its pace deceived the batsman, but because the batsman wanted to make it so clear that he was not deceived – by placing the ball out of the ground – that he succumbed to excess of energy, from sheer resentment at the idea of such a ball deceiving him. Of course, however, it must be remembered that there are batsmen who consider every slow ball must be full of guile and be treated with the most canny respect. In the same way men make their own difficulties in more important matters than cricket.

So Tom Hunter came with his little skips to the crease and, bowing his head, delivered the ball with sudden fury at the imperturbable Jim Stevens, who awaited the onslaught with calm and confidence. The ball came straight at his legs, a good length, and Jim intended to play it back to the bowler, but it struck the edge and not the centre of his bat and glanced smartly off in the direction of Ted Bannister, who watched its course with the utmost composure, then gathered himself together to run after it, overtook it as it ceased to roll, and over-ran it, then returned, stooping, and taking many little steps to show his keenness, wound himself valiantly up and flung the ball back to the wicket, much pleased with his exhibition of fielding, while poor Gauvinier cursed and fumed, and the batsman ran a comfortable couple, making a mental note that there was always a run to leg.

'A fellow like that lets the whole side down,' the poor captain internally groaned, and old John McLeod, noticing the black look on his face, thought that Mr. Gauvinier should make greater allowance for age and possible infirmity, since the good Ted was so obviously doing his best.

Young Horace Cairie glared at Mr. Bannister in a way that ill became his tender years.

Waite lolled at cover as though to show that he was not accustomed to be fielding on the same side as men like that leg fieldsman whom he did not recognise as the man he had spotted as a possible batsman, and yet that he was able to accommodate himself to the spirit of any game. In consequence, he was unprepared for Jim Stevens' next shot, and stumbled as he ran forward to collect the ball, and his effort to run the batsmen out who were stealing a run was completely unsuccessful. He flung the ball wide of Jim Saddler at the wicket and there was an overthrow. He was cricketer enough to be very annoyed at this clumsiness, and pulled himself together to be ready if the chance came, to show that he realised the importance of keen fielding. Howls of derision came from the small boys: and shouts of excited encouragement from the Raveley players.

Old John McLeod, at point, was not exactly glad to see Waite's error, but yet he was not wholly sorry.

Tom Hunter thought to himself: 'That's just the sort of luck I should have!' and delivered the next ball with ferocity, rather short on the off, which Jim Stevens hit at and struck towards point. Old John with amazing agility jumped with outstretched arm and stopped it with his stout hand, but, alas! his prayer was unanswered, the ball did not stick in it, and he did not bring off the catch of his life, though it was a feat to have stopped the ball at all – a feat, too, greeted by applause from players and spectators alike.

Goodness! If he had only managed to hold the dratted thing and show toffs from London and others that he could do a bit of fielding, even if he couldn't show 'em he was a good judge of a run.

Maria having heard the contact of the ball upon her husband's palm (it sounded loud as the smack of her own loving hand upon a baby's bottom), almost screamed, fearing that one at least of his dear fingers must be broken. No; she never would understand the pleasure of a game of cricket, knowing how dangerously hard a cricket ball was.

'Plenty of luck I get; all bad,' thought Tom Hunter, though he had called out as loudly as anyone upon the field: 'Well stopped, sir!' in appreciation of old John's keenness and agility. 'The old fellow is a real, genuine sportsman,' Waite thought without the least trace of patronage, for, underneath his Beckenham manner, he, too, was a genuine sportsman: and so was Tom Hunter, somewhere deep underneath his manifold prickles.

An innings often opens a little shakily, as though 'the luck' were wondering on which side to settle. Usually the shakiness is seen on the batting side in these swift half-day matches; and their main effort seems not to be 'got on the run' and be jollied out for a depressing total before they had fully realised that the batting had really begun. But on this occasion two dropped catches, though neither were easy and one had been supremely difficult, and two bits of bad fielding (one, alas! habitual and the other most exceptional) put such heart and confidence into the batsmen that they felt forty had been scored rather than four. Their perkiness, however (felt by the fieldsmen rather than observed), set the Tillingfold side on their toes (all, that is to say, except Ted Bannister, who maintained his usual unswerving composure), and Gauvinier, during the next few overs, was aware of the good tenseness of the contest thrilling through himself and his men (with one bland exception). He knew that it was going to be a good game, and that it was unlikely a 'rot' would suddenly set in, however surprising the changes in cricket may be. 'Early days yet! Early days yet!' he said to himself. 'Anything may happen.'

Eager little Joe Stonor had scored two singles and Jim Stevens one, a pleasant drive off Sid which Trine had been glad to receive, as it made the hope of a catch less distant, when Sid gave a confident appeal for l.b.w. off the eager little wicket-keeper, which the Raveley umpire stolidly declined to allow. Sid never appealed unless he was quite sure that the man was out, and he was much annoyed, sportsman as he was, at the decision. To work off his annoyance, which was not lessened by Joe's ill-concealed satisfaction, he swung in his fastest ball, which became a yorker just outside the leg stump, and Jim Saddler, thinking that it would hit the wicket, failed to get his legs behind it; and the ball went for two byes.

So the score crept slowly up, run by run, to nineteen, and both batsmen remained undefeated, at which point Tom Hunter sent down a bad long hop – his first really bad ball – to Jim Stevens, who pulled it easily to the boundary, the first four in the Raveley innings.

Tom Hunter had been bowling very well, yet twenty-three was up. Gauvinier wondered if he should give him one more over or take him off now. Two or three more loose balls like that last one and the score would soon pass thirty. It was time a wicket fell.

Sid, no longer in the mood for banter, sent down a maiden over. He was bowling for all he was worth, and though he could not get much work on the ball owing to the state of the ground, he kept the batsmen well in hand, by the way in which he varied his pace. You felt that he could go on bowling like that all the innings without tiring or losing his length; and so he could – and cheerfully would – Gauvinier knew.

'Try another, Tom,' he said. 'Your luck'll change this over.'

'Or it may *not*,' Tom answered, glad that he was going to have another chance of getting Jim Steven's wicket.

But again, in his anxiety to bowl a faster ball than he could, he sent down that deplorable long hop on Jim's body which again Jim hooked without difficulty to the boundary.

'Three more of those,' thought Gauvinier in some dismay, 'and they'll be nearing fifty for no wickets.'

A set and anxious look became visible on the faces of the Tillingfold side. Matters were looking serious.

Tom grew reckless, and as his fastest ball was a failure, determined to deliver his slowest, and did so. Jim Stevens felt that touch of resentment which this slow one was apt to excite in certain batsmen, and had a tremendous go at it; as though merely to put it out of the ground would in no way ease his feelings; to do that the ball must at least reach that distant region known as Kingdom Come. He sprang out and hit mightily, but mis-hit, and the ball rose soaring, not into the next field but one, but straight up high and higher, and poor Dick Fanshawe, knowing that it was his catch and fearing Tom Hunter or Waite might try for it, uttered a lugubrious 'Mine' and ran back, gazing up and up, and at the last moment, as he could not run backwards fast enough and was afraid to turn and run forward and try the catch over his shoulder, made a stumbling dive for the ball, which struck his fingers, indeed, but was not held. It would have been a good catch to make: it was a horrible catch to miss. *D'affreux désespoirs d'un instant:* the ghastly despairs of a moment. The words sounded in his mind like a knell of doom as he cursed his own clumsy slowness and muttered: 'Oh, sorry, Tom!' in tragic tones, as he tossed the accursed ball back to the bowler. His middle finger was rather badly bruised, but he paid no heed to that in the general soreness of his pride and his feelings.

And only the evening before he had held every catch – among them some beauties – which had been knocked up at practice. To him now the match was irreparably lost, and all through his own stupid, bungling fault. He was not the man to let himself off at all; on the contrary he rubbed the salt bitterness well into his wound, gaining a grim satisfaction from the sting. Consolation was offered to him from every side; but he knew that a decent cricketer would have made certain of such a catch as that – every time. He did not even feel a decent man, let alone a decent cricketer.

They had run, too, and the score was now twenty-eight for no wickets, with Slater, that redoubtable hitter, still to bat.

But now the imp of fortune, who delights to sway the destiny of men and of cricketers, fluttered across from one side to the other: an imp of mischief in this case, bringing judgment on Gauvinier for his impatience with his largest, most benignant fieldsman. For after a steady maiden over from Sid, with whom Jim Stevens, set as he was, could take no liberty, Gauvinier went on to bowl himself in place of Tom Hunter, who went off reluctantly, considering well the catches that had been missed off his bowling and forgetting his loose balls.

Gauvinier noticed that for some time Ted Bannister had been edging nearer and nearer the wicket to save himself a walk at the change of over, blandly oblivious, as always, of the importance of standing in the right place: and he was now seven or eight yards too near the wicket. Gauvinier had, as a matter of fact, called out a suggestion to him that he should move farther back, but the call had only evoked a pleasant smile and a shuffle of the feet. Nothing would have kept the good Ted in his right place short of leading him there by his large hand and marking the spot with a feather or some conspicuous object. Gauvinier had aroused adverse criticism in early days of his captaincy by resorting to this procedure: now there was enough general keenness to make it unnecessary. But the sight of Bannister must have had some subtle influence on the poor captain, because his first ball was a fast half volley wide of the leg stump, which the eager little Joe swept round and hit – hit full and straight – for the portly centre of the astonished Ted, who, too near to avoid the cruel impact, hastily, with terror on his face, bending up, put both large hands to ward off injury and held the ball to save his life, and eager little Joe was out.

Gauvinier became almost hysterical in his effort to congratulate Ted upon the catch with proper seriousness; for he had noticed the look of terror on his face as the ball flew towards his portly middle, and the look of bland satisfaction and surprise (not at all overdone) which took terror's place, as soon as he realised that the catch had been made.

Old John, his firm belief in his friend now solidly established for ever, saw nothing humorous whatever in the incident, and hurried up to him and beat him upon the back, saying fervently:

'Oh, well held, Ted, well held: magnificent catch! Magnificent catch!'

Horace Cairie, wild with glee, danced about singing out: 'Oh, golly, he's held it! Oh, golly, he's held it!'

And Sid, looking at him in what used to be called a quizzical fashion, said: 'Well, didn't you expect him to, then?'

Thus was Ted Bannister's reputation as a fine fieldsman made among a large number of the less judicious cricket enthusiasts in Tillingfold; and Gauvinier had small ground left for his tentative hints that Ted Bannister should be omitted from the team on occasions when Tillingfold were playing a strong side.

Gauvinier was a good medium-paced bowler, whom Sam Bird and other cricket worthies often expressed a wish to see pitted against a really good batting side. But they would have been disappointed, probably, had their wish been realised, for the Tillingfold captain could never bowl well unless he were supported by the full keenness of his side. High-class club cricket, where individual prowess takes the place of this general keenness, left him, as the Americans say, tired. On his day, when Tillingfold were in a tight place, he often bowled with deadly effect, and in the surrounding villages he was well known and feared. One set in the village declared, in spite of figures, that there was nothing in his bowling; that it was ordinary, straightforward stuff that needed hitting; but they showed obtuseness to the delicacies of pitch and variation of pace and of the slight break from the leg which sends a catch into the slips off the shoulder of the bat.

Tom Hunter belonged to this set, as, indeed, to many grousing others; and his internal comment on Gauvinier's first wicket, amply justified in this case, was: 'Just like his bloomin' luck!' and he felt rather uneasy in his mind when Gauvinier, who well knew Tom's opinion of his bowling powers, came up to him and said, smiling: 'Just like my luck, Tom, isn't it?' and calling out 'Tri-ine,' pitched the ball hard and high for a catch to young Trine in the deep, who, holding it, jerked it to Waite, who, hearing Horrie's clamour, threw him a smart one, which the boy was glad to hold.

Dick Fanshawe walked gloomily up to Gauvinier and said in a sepulchral voice: 'I am sorry I fumbled that catch, Polly.'

'Oh! It was a stinker. Anyone might have dropped it. Running back like that, you know, when the ground is none too even.'

Dick smiled, totally unconvinced, and as he returned to his place Sid, laughing, tossed him a very easy catch, asking him why he had not wiped the butter from his fingers after his tea.

'If our captain were worth his salt he'd go round with his handkerchief and see to that little matter for some of us.' And he turned to Horrie, who was buckled up with laughter and general pleasure at the fall of the first wicket, to say very solemnly: 'If ever you gets to be a captain, my son, never forget to keep a large red handkerchief. . . .' But he was interrupted by Dick, stirred out of his gloom, coming up to assault him. 'Now then,' Sid cried, 'I won't have it. Fightin's not allowed on the field. Ask Horrie there!'

Meanwhile the young gentleman who kept race-horses had made his way to the wicket, and Teddie White, who knew that he kept race-horses, felt a kind of reflected glory in fielding when such a man was actually batting. It brought him beautifully near to his hobby, a little nearer, perhaps, than he had ever before been to a race-horse. Had that accursed 'busman really forgotten to put his half-crown on *Shake-your-Heels?* It was a painful question that would often repeat itself in his mind and would never receive a satisfactory answer.

The young gentleman clearly meant business, and he lashed out at Gauvinier's first ball in a way which caused the fieldsmen to expect a merry time. But he missed it, and the ball, rising with unexpected quickness, had poor Jim Saddler out, because the previous secretary, when the matter had been brought up at a Committee Meeting, had considered that a wicket-keeper's shield was, after all, rather a funny thing to write for to a stranger, though at the meeting, his modesty being dormant, he had cheerfully consented to procure one at Gauvinier's earnest suggestion. Since then the matter had lapsed, and so poor Jim Saddler was stretched out on the ground, and Maria, seing a man hurt, was chiefly thankful that the man was not her dear husband, though she was, of course, sorry that any man should be hurt. Still, the man not being John, she could be cool and philosophic and think that if they would choose to play with a hard ball instead of a nice soft one, they must put up with any injuries caused by their masculine obstinacy and wilfulness. Deep within her there was something which never failed, much as she loved and respected her husband, to regard all men as essentially babies. She was, metaphorically speaking, always ready with a pocket handkerchief with which to wipe their little wet noses.

Jim Saddler struggled to his feet and took his stand once more, after a respectful round of applause, behind the stumps. The young gentleman drove the next ball hard and fast along the ground towards Horrie at mid-on, who leapt out and stopped it with his right hand, an alert and plucky piece of fielding which the Raveley men cheered from the Pavilion, and many of his own side from the ground, while Horace was too keen and pleased at stopping it to hear a sound. His confidence, after his decent innings and after not fumbling any yet in the field, was delightfully growing. It wouldn't be his fault, he swore, if any passed him. And his mother, who had returned from tea and was now watching, did hope that he would be careful. Cooh! He hardly felt the bruise on his thigh at all except when he pressed it. Little Oliver, doleful after seeing his adored father miss a catch (which he tried loyally to convince himself no one at all could possibly have caught), yelled with joy at his hero's prowess.

The old, old man from his favourite seat in front of the Pavilion announced to no one in particular: 'I do like to see a young one slippy in the field. That's a good little lad, that is; a good little lad.' And memory took him back with all the ease imaginable to the many, many years ago when he himself was a keen little nipper, playing among men, winning his spurs; took him back (so strong is the power of fellow-feeling) so vividly and so swiftly and so completely that, could he have caught a glimpse of himself, he would not have recognised as himself the queer, bent, wrinkled, fattish chap on the bench, old now, so old.

Waite had the next one; slap at him along the ground, and he gathered and returned it in style. Gauvinier, with his skipper's sensibility, felt the whole side braced and expectant and eager to win (even the one exception had been stung by the catch out of his usual bland composure), and he revelled, rejoicing, in the good feeling that emanates from eleven men joined together for a common end. And all the men forgot themselves and were happy in this good feeling, the most tonic healthful feeling that exists.

What wise old poet wrote

> Joy's a subtil elf;
> I think man's happiest when he forgets himself?

He knew what he was writing about, whoever he may have been.

Pethering, the young gentleman who kept race-horses, was playing vigorously and well, and he hit hard and straight at Gauvinier's next ball, a good-length ball, but he was deceived by the slight leg break, and the ball, touching only the edge of the bat, flew off into the slips, where Sid Smith, leaping out, his big safe hand stretched well out, brought off a magnificent catch.

Immense jubilation greeted this feat and this turning of the Tillingfold luck. Thirty odd for two good wickets looked far more comfortable than thirty odd for no wickets.

Dick Fanshawe joined the little crowd round Sid and, lifting his big hand, said it was hardly fair to bring a pair of that size on to the field.

'That's what I always tell him,' Teddie White remarked. 'Like bloomin' great nets. A ball couldn't very well help gettin' caught in a thing like that.'

'As good a catch, that, as you could see anywhere,' said Waite, with the authority of several county grounds behind him.

'First rate!' said Ted Bannister. 'But the sort I hates most is the one that comes straight into your body, like.'

Gauvinier turned away, coughing.

'No choice about them,' he heard Sid gravely remark. 'You've got to catch 'em or be destroyed.'

'Yes, exactly; you're so in your own light, so to speak, and so infernally tied up.'

'Man in! called out Gauvinier, full of marvel and delight at the incomparable Ted Bannister; wondering, too, how many people on the ground were aware that one catch had been an egregious, ridiculous fluke, and that the other had been the reward of skill and watchfulness and a quite remarkable aptitude for the position of short slip. It somehow added to the enchantment of the game to have a cricketer like Sid Smith and a cricketer like Ted Bannister on the same side.

'Well, I'll be jiggered!' thought Tom Hunter, 'if the chap hasn't got two lucky wickets in his first over!'

The excitement was growing more intense now two men were out. A sort of desperation is apt to come over spectators in a village match when the first batsmen slowly, but surely, pile up the tens; it seems impossible that a wicket could ever fall. Now many veered over to the other extreme and felt positive that Raveley would be lucky to score fifty. 'Got 'em on the run now!' was the confident thought in their minds.

Therefore it was a shock to them when Garfield, the next man in, despatched the last ball of Gauvinier's over to the leg boundary with the ease and precision of a man who has been batting for hours. The Raveley men greeted the stroke with roars of delight because they were sensitive to the general atmosphere, and the shot let light into it.

Old John remembered that Jim Stevens was not yet out; that Slater had not yet come in, and that a year or two ago, Garfield, going in last but one, had helped himself to twenty in two overs. He had come on, too, as a bat since then; and there were two or three other Raveley men – Boyes and Hammond and Smart, for instance – who took a bit of shifting on their day; and it was no use denying it; it was not a bowler's wicket.

Jim Stevens knocked Sid's first ball out towards deep mid-wicket, where Teddie White, well drawn now into the game and oblivious of 'busmen or horses, by sheer alacrity saved two, which the batsmen in crossing had agreed to take. ('No, no!' they shouted and withdrew.) And Garfield faced Sid. He, resolved to waste no time, hit Sid hard and high towards young Trine, but wide of him to the off, and young Trine, going at full speed, regardless of the rough ground and longish grass, all out for the catch, reached the ball with his right hand and nearly as possible brought off a magnificent catch and actually brought off a magnificent try: but they scored two runs.

The excitement was growing, and it was well for many small boys that the pace slowed down a little, for Sid finished his over without having any more hits off him, and his last ball but one, at which Garfield had a go, shaved his wicket, so that Jim Saddler cursed under his breath and Sid eased his feelings by slapping his thigh.

Gauvinier, strung up tight in every nerve, took a maiden over off Jim Stevens, whom no excitement could lure into taking liberties, but the last ball beat him for pace, and came near enough to the off stump to make Sid Smith smile his slow smile, as who should say: 'They've not got it quite all their own way yet.'

The maiden over tried Garfield's patience; he was anxious to put up the fifty and to lower the number of runs that separated his side from the coveted hundred and three.

He stepped valiantly out at Sid's first ball and hit him hard and very high this time, not wide of young Trine in the deep, and Trine, moving without hurry, got nicely underneath the ball and held the catch, and was awfully pleased to hold it, and the whole Tillingfold side and all the Tillingfold supporters were awfully pleased to see him hold it.

'Cooh! Straight into his hands!' said young Oliver, after emitting a yell of delight. 'My dad had to run back miles, and he bossed one when he had to run much less.'

'A juicy one!' said young Trine, coming up to Sid. 'Saw it all the way. *You* know.' And he was grinning with pleasure.

'I thought we ought to get him between us,' Sid answered beaming.

There was no disparity at all between the two men now. They were just two men in flannels, with no little history attaching to their trousers, and yet on Monday evening Trine would be unable to understand Sid's rather surly salute, as he returned, a bricklayer's cad, to his wife and family; and he himself rode his chestnut mare home to change for dinner. 'Damn it!' he would think to himself, 'I don't despise him for being a working man!' But then young Trine had always knocked off an hour or two before he felt half as dog tired as Sid would then be feeling.

And still Slater did not come in. Boyes, a youth about twenty, keen and strong, was making his quick way to the wicket. Somehow, this diffidence on the part of the Raveley captain was rather disconcerting; it suggested an unpleasant reserve of strength on the batting side. Boyes, too, seemed cool and unhurried; he played Sid without alarm, and put away his last ball for two runs in a matter-of-fact manner that dismayed the heart of little Horace Cairie, who thought that, after all, Sid liked a softer wicket, and that he had been bowling quite a long time and only taken one wicket.

Slowly the score reached fifty; a run here, a run there, a bye; a leg bye. The bowlers kept the game well in hand; the runs were fought for; but one by one they were gained. Then suddenly Boyes, no longer able to restrain himself, stepped out and hit Gauvinier clean out of the ground for six.

'Oh, mum, they're winning!' moaned Oliver, hiding his face, unashamed, in his mother's lap, and though they managed to hide their feelings more successfully than Oliver, it must be owned that many on the field shared his forlorn opinion. If their tails could have been seen they would have been observed to be lowered. The strain was beginning to tell. And black dismay descended upon the Tillingfold team when Boyes, misjudging the flight of the next ball, scooped a simple catch to Bannister, who fumbled it grossly. A shout of horrid triumph came from the Pavilion. Dick Fanshawe tried to arouse in his heart fellow-feeling for Ted Bannister; but without success. The egregious Ted seemed to think that it was rather funny to drop a catch at this stage of the game. What Gauvinier muttered may not be written down. But he called out in a loud voice: 'Bad luck! Bad luck!' and sent down his fastest ball, which Boyes hit hard towards Horace and started to run. Horace, jumping out, reached the ball and flung it back so hard that it stung Jim Saddler's hand through his thick gloves. If Boyes had not been nimble he would have been run out.

Waite shouted out from cover: 'Well fielded, young 'un!' He was feeling the rich tensity of the game and enjoying it.

The smartness and keenness of the boy gave Gauvinier just that little extra something which enabled him to send down his slowish ball, risking six or a wicket, and Boyes ran out to hit and missed and the ball removed his off bail neatly, daintily.

'Oh, well bowled!' came the yell of joy from many men on the field and many spectators, and small boys whistled and punched each other and uttered cat-calls.

Now at length Slater, clapped by his own men, came towards the wicket, and Gauvinier, seeing him emerge, called out: 'Left hand,' for the Raveley captain bowled with his right arm and batted left-handed.

It was necessary for third man to become leg and leg to become third man. Gauvinier from long experience abandoned any hope of getting Ted Bannister into the right place; he relied upon Sid at short slip to help him to approximate to it and asked old John to stand deeper a little behind the wicket. On his day Slater could drive hard, and he had the left-hander's pull to perfection: a dangerous man, as most of the players knew: a good man to see the back of, when runs were wanted: a horrid man to get out, for he could rise to an occasion such as the present. But he started shakily, being far too late for his first ball and only just coming down on the next, which kept low, in time.

Attention was so rivetted on Slater, and Jim Stevens' presence at the wicket had become such an accepted fact, that it was a queer surprise to everyone when Sid Smith clean bowled the imperturbable Jim with the second ball of his over. The pause between the wicket's fall and the applause of the spectators marked the extent of the surprise. They looked at the score-board – five wickets for fifty-six, last man twenty-two – with only Slater, who might make a few, to get out, why, the match was as good as won. Gauvinier, feeling the tenseness evaporate, feared the awful snare of over-confidence, and remarked to Jim Saddler that a match was never won until the last wicket had fallen. Waite, joining the group, supposed they'd got it well in hand now.

At which Dick Fanshawe said rather angrily: 'You never know!' angry that Waite should not sufficiently see the danger of over-confidence, and Waite wondered why the fellow who seemed a good enough sort of chap should have such a surly manner.

Bill Hammond was the next batsman, a little, wiry bricklayer, with large ears and a bushy moustache, who had been playing cricket regularly for nearer fifty than forty years and liked a game with something in it.

'I'll stop 'em and you can hit,' he said jovially to Slater, and Sid, who knew him of old, asked: 'Sure you will, Bill?'

'We'll say so Sid, at any rate,' he cheerfully threw back.

And anyone could see that he had played a lot of cricket by the way in which he shaped at Sid's first ball, which he watched like a cat and played without hesitation.

Nor, apparently, was the game old fellow going to be content with merely stopping them, for he hit a ball on the leg stump which Sid intended to be a yorker, for a good two, and ran, so that old John McLeod envied his wind and wiriness and pace.

Slater remained shaky for some time, but the score crept up to sixty – then sixty-one, sixty-two, sixty-three – and, as he remarked to Jim Saddler behind the stumps, peony-red with excitement and anxiety to stop byes, 'A miss is as good as a mile – every time.' And at length came an over in which he hit Sid hard and full for three fours, boundaries which young Trine, stretch and spring as he might, could not possibly save, and the score stood at seventy-five; twenty-eight to tie; twenty-nine to win.

Should he take the terrible risk, Gauvinier anxiously wondered, of taking off the reliable Sid and trying Tom Hunter in the hope of snatching a wicket by a change? No: one more over for Sid, and in that over Slater helped himself to two more fours; twenty-one to win: and, judging by the howls of joy from the Pavilion, those twenty-one runs were as good as made. Still Gauvinier waited for a wicket to fall in his own over before changing Sid for Tom Hunter: and he did not wait in vain, for Bill Hammond struck out at a ball on the off, and old John at point, in spite of his years and rotundity, shot out his fat hand as he sprang and, though he overbalanced and fell quite a thump, he held the ball. The applause drowned a little suppressed scream from Maria, who, however, decided that she had had quite enough of it, and went off into the village to make her purchases for the evening jollification – purchases to which she now added mentally a fresh bottle of embrocation. She tossed her head as fiercely as she could, to wonder for the thousandth time how it was possible for sensible, full-grown men of John's age to get so excited about a game of ball: and that,

too (Oh, woman! Oh, woman!), when six wickets were down and only twenty runs wanted for a draw.

Five more fours from Slater, thought Horace in an agony of excitement, fuming against Smart, the next Raveley batsman, for not hastening to the wicket. At length, however, Smart arrived at the wicket, just as the church clock struck 6.30, and it passed through Horrie's mind that all the team except Slater had now decided to play for a draw: if Slater could hit the runs off, well and good: they preferred to take no risk and play out time. Something like this may have been the case, but Horace was unjust to denounce them as utterly unsportsmanlike swine.

Gauvinier's first ball Smart mis-hit towards Ted Bannister, and Slater, knowing his man, took the first run at a fearful pace and forced Smart to a second, which he took quite safely while the large, abominable Ted trod his little dance and wound himself up for the throw.

'Now you've got him: at the wicket!' yelled Gauvinier, beside himself, wasting his breath. Smart was behind the wicket before the ball rolled in to Jim Saddler.

Nineteen to win.

Smart played softly, carefully forward at the next ball, and hit it softly up well out of the reach of any but a passionately keen mid-on. But Horace, on his little toes, watching every ball on to the bat and off it, came tearing up and, flinging himself at full length underneath the ball, brought off an extraordinary catch, the intensity of his determination to get to the ball being almost amusing. Smart looked amazed at the prostrate boy, not realising at first that he was out; but slowly the melancholy fact

dawned upon him, and muttering: 'Well, I'll be damned!' he began his retreat to the Pavilion.

'Bravo, young 'un! that's the sort of fielding that wins matches,' Waite called, his Beckenham manner entirely changed now into bright-eyed keenness, and walking up to Trine he said: 'There's a lot in what you say about these village games. The actual standard of cricket mayn't be. . . . Just listen to those kids. . . . Godfrey Daniel, I've not felt like this since my first school match . . . well, hardly.'

And now the old catch, to the tune of the church chimes, broke out again round the ground in steady earnest:

'Play up, Tillingfold; play up, Tillingfold.'

And Gauvinier, walking up to Slater said: 'Something like a game.'

And the Raveley captain answered: 'That's a fact!'

The whole team were now playing together like one good, keen man. Tom Hunter forgot his grievances and hoped that Gauvinier wouldn't change the bowling, though he wouldn't mind having a go himself if he *were* wanted: old John could look at Waite without any feeling of resentment, and was oblivious of his little undervest: Dick Fanshawe saw in young Trine not a sprig of what he most hated, but a fellow-sportsman who was perservering in the deep; *Shake-your-Heels* was a dim phantom memory to Teddie White; Jim Saddler almost wished that Bill Bannock were playing in his stead, if that would mean fewer byes. They were all happy and keen and good-tempered in their great united effort to win the match; for half an hour they would be as alive and alert as men should always be, and Gauvinier was certain that good old Ted Bannister was doing his level best, though he prayed earnestly that no ball might come his cumbersome way.

Sid Smith came up to him and said: 'How about trying Tom for an over this end? Slater's rather got the hang of me.'

Gauvinier looked dubious.

'A change works wonders sometimes.'

'Four or five fours, you know . . . and we're done.'

'Ask him.'

They walked up to Tom.

'How do you feel about an over Sid's end, Tom?'

'Don't mind trying!' said Tom, awfully pleased.

'If you take a wicket, I'll probably put Sid on again, because he's deadly on the tail.'

'Oh, I understand,' Tom eagerly agreed, thinking at the moment: 'Jolly nice chap, the boss!'

'Man in! Come on!'

'Centre!' called the umpire, Sam Bird. 'One to come.'

Nothing happened. Mercer, the new Raveley batsman, stopped it.

Tom Hunter took the ball, determined to bowl better than he had ever bowled in his life before: but his first ball to the left-handed Slater (he was put off at bowling to a left-hander) was that horrible fast long hop on the body, which Slater pulled clean out of the ground for a terrific six. Five more balls to come in that over; thirteen more runs to win. The shouts of the Raveley team sounded harsh and clangorous and rude against the awful silence of the Tillingfold supporters: chi-ikes, too, of gleeful derision greeted the next ball, which Slater pulled for four by the gate leading into the road. Tom Hunter felt desperate. Four more balls to come in that pernicious over. He simply ran up to the wicket and bowled without thought or intention except, somehow, to get the over finished; Slater appeared a fell demon who could do anything with a bat twice the width of the wickets, light as straw, powerful as an infernal machine. Tom saw him hit out again, but did not see the ball fly straight at Dick Fanshawe, who grimly stretched up a rigid, fearless hand from which the ball bounced slowly back, to be caught by his two hands, a catch of desperate, painful resolution.

It was the turn of the Tillingfold small boys, and they took it, not forgetting, however, to pay the Raveley captain the tribute of his pluck, or the Raveley men in the Pavilion the tribute of their late jeering.

'Ninety-five – eight – thirty-five,' called out old Francis from his perch in the score-box. 'That's eight to tie and nine to win and twenty more minutes to go. And if this don't end pretty soon,' he added under his breath to the Raveley scorer, who was gnawing his pencil ferociously, 'I shall charge the cricket club with a new pair of trousers.'

'He sometimes puts those two in first to break the bowling!' remarked the little scorer.

'Here, now, don't give us a bad 'eart, matey, damn it!'

'Well, it's a fact, he do!' said his colleague, far too tightly strung up to laugh.

Maiden followed maiden amid a tense silence! Tom, having gained his wicket, gave way to Sid, who could be relied upon to put down no loose ball; a leg bye was shrilly cheered, a bye acclaimed like a six. The church clock had struck a quarter to seven. The Raveley batsmen were hanging desperately on. The excitement became feverish when Sid Smith fell over in trying to stop a bye and in his anxiety to run the batsman out, hurled the ball in hard and too high and gave away an overthrow. A flick to leg which Ted Bannister saved from being two (fielding *incognito*, as it were, to the present men) and the hundred went up, amid prolonged applause from the Raveley men standing now in eager groups outside the Pavilion.

Sid set his teeth. The strain was becoming almost unbearable, and with his last ball he knocked down the middle stump of the wicket.

Seven more minutes to go; three runs for a tie! four a win. The Tillingfold men spoke little, but waited, anxious for the arrival of the last man, whom Slater had run into the Pavilion to hurry up, ignoring the few cries that insisted on taking the full legal two minutes. The umpires produced their watches.

Off the first ball Jim Saddler with a shriek appealed for a catch at the wicket, hearing a flick, but Sam Bird declined to allow it.

'Play the game, Tillingfold,' came an angry shout from the Pavilion, which poor Jim Saddler heard, and was so distressed to hear that he let the next ball pass him for a bye, which would have been two but for Sid's smartness and the batsmen's hesitation.

Another terrible maiden followed, in which the ball shaved that lucky last man's wicket on either side, as though the ball were bewitched or inspired to see how near it could go to the wicket without touching it.

The fielders ran to their places to save time, perhaps, for one more over. Sid bowled another maiden.

Sam Bird, looking at his watch, called out: 'Last over!'

Gauvinier tried his fastest ball; that last man played it resolutely back. He tried a slowish yorker; that last man blocked it all of a sudden at the last second. He tried a nice, good-length ball, hoping for a slight break from the leg; that last man played forward, missed it, and the ball broke too much and missed the off stump by three or four inches. He tried another of the same kind; that last man played forward again, the ball hit the shoulder of his bat and Sid, with a yell, secured it and hurled it as high into the air as he could pitch it, and Gauvinier shouted: 'Well caught, Sid!' so loud that his voice broke, and he started coughing.

The match was over, won by two runs, on time.

The match was over . . . the stumps had been pulled . . . players and spectators straggled up the road in thick gossiping throngs.

Chapter Eight

THE EVENING PASSES AND NIGHT FALLS

The stumps had been pulled up and stored with the umpire's torn coats in the locker; the seats and benches had been carried into the Pavilion; the large shutters had been lowered; the doors of the Pavilion barred and locked. The cricket ground, in the light of the sinking sun, looked as desolate as the two worn patches by the bowlers' creases, which were now the only visible signs that a match had been played.

Players and spectators straggled up the road to the village in thick, gossiping throngs, through which young Trine in his two-seater (giving Waite a lift) slowly made his way, tooting his horn and wishing 'Good-night' to players and others whom he knew, at any rate, by sight. Sid Smith met his wife and children at the gate and persuaded her to come back into the village to listen to the band, which would play that evening in the Square. Keen eyes of women gave Mrs. Sid three months before her next came; but there, you could never be certain! In her best clothes and in his own happy humour after the match Sid had a glimpse of the fine lass, Liz, he had wooed before the swamp of domesticity had closed over their heads. He pushed the perambulator up the hill in the vain but valiant hope of regaining that girl, a hope that glimmered dimly and dumbly in some remote corner of his consciousness.

Old John, Ted Bannister and Teddie White slowed up as they came to 'The Dog and Duck.' Old John, in a more benevolent mood even than usual, was much affected by the sight of the small family party, Sid pushing the pram, with two small boys hanging on to his jacket. He came hurrying up to Mrs. Smith:

'You must let your husband join us,' he said. 'We've had such a glorious nice match; the best match as I've ever played in, I do verily believe.'

All smiles, Mrs. Sid answered: 'Now don't you keep him long, Mr. McLeod, mind.'

'Long, bless me, no, Mrs. Smith! But your good man'll be parched as a day in the desert.'

'Oh no! That's all right; I'll stay here,' said Sid, protesting. But Ted Bannister took one arm and old John the other, and he was dragged into 'The Dog and Duck,' not, it must be owned, too reluctantly. A friendly but vigorous argument ensued between John and Ted Bannister as to who should stand treat, which was won by Ted Bannister, John grumbling that he never knew such a chap.

'Go on, put that inside yourself, mate,' said Ted, handing him a pint of old Burton, for which 'The Dog and Duck' had a name.

Nothing is quite so refreshing as a long, cool drink of good old ale after a hot afternoon's cricket; each man took a long, appreciative draught after wishing each other, 'Well, here's luck!' and then in silence allowed the pleasant effect of that drink to permeate quietly through him before enjoying another good pull at the big pewter mug. John's face was a study of happy comfort as he slowly tilted his pot and, emptying it, set it down on the counter, carefully drawing a deep, comfortable sigh. Beaming, he watched the others follow his excellent example and then said, as though inspired by a sudden novel idea of extreme brilliancy:

'How about another small one?'

The men smiled. In a most businesslike manner John asked Jock, the barman, for another half-pint each, and over that the men, their first parched thirst a little quenched, were able to chat. They discussed the great question who had really done the most to win the match for Tillingfold, and after dismissing the claims, first of one man, then of another, came to the conclusion that every man on the side had done his share.

'Ah! that's the beauty of cricket!' declared old John heartily, wiping his face all over with a large handkerchief, 'that's the glorious beauty of cricket. Every single man-jack of us helped, one way or another – to win that game.'

'Yes!' said Ted Bannister, with the utmost composure: 'if there is a better game than cricket I should like to know it.' And he surveyed the company as a man does who has said the last word.

What would have been Gauvinier's thoughts had he heard him say it?

'If there is a better game than cricket I should like to know it,'
said Ted Bannister, with the utmost composure.

Gauvinier, as a matter of fact, was quietly absorbing with Francis Allen, the scorer, a tap of old beer which he preferred to that to be obtained at 'The Dog and Duck.' The pub was at the end of the village, more retired perhaps and secluded.

'It adds to the life of the place, a game like that, this afternoon –' said Gauvinier. 'It'll be a pity if we can't get another field for football, and cricket should have to stop. The turf must have a rest.'

'Yes, it's just not going proper-like since the war.'

'All the grousing and chat really is only a sign of keenness, don't you think?'

'No use payin' any heed to that, man,' said old Francis encouragingly, pouring his beer down.

'I wonder why one is so mad on cricket. It's only a game, after all.'

'Here! you'd better have another half-pint to wash that duck of yours off your chest.'

He ordered it, while Paul laughed.

'I'd like to have made a few to-day. Your young Horace batted well. He should be a fine cricketer one day.'

'They're nice people, the whole lot of 'em,' said Francis, appreciatively. 'The nipper wanted to play to-day – just a little. I had some fun with 'un this morning.' He paused, savouring the reminiscence. 'Wouldn't let on I had a message for 'un. He pretty nigh bust hisself wanting to know.'

'The kid's not an atom conceited. I'd as soon have him on a side as any man I've ever played with.'

Francis looked very pleased.

'Except, perhaps, Mr. Waite, eh? or Ted Bannister,' he slyly suggested.

'You are an old devil. Who's ever told you. . . .'

'Who's told me! You hide yer blummin' feelings too well.'

'Oh, damn it! I try to,' said Gauvinier guiltily. 'But that catch . . .' He began to shake with laughter.

'Pretty near scared the life out of him! Mind now, or you'll spill the beer over your trousies. I could see his scared look from the score-box.'

Gauvinier managed to finish his beer without a catastrophe.

'The joke is that half Tillingfold will think him a class fielder now.'

'Well, why not?'

'Oh, no reason, of course, only it's rather funny. So damnably like the world.'

'It takes all sorts to make a world, if it comes to that.'

'You're right, Francis, you're right. One's little job is to find the place for the Bannocks and the Bannisters, that's all.'

There was a silence.

'Oh well!' said Gauvinier, 'I must push along, I suppose.'

'Yes, mustn't sit here all the evening makin' beasts of our selves.'

They slowly 'got a move on,' and Gauvinier mounted his bicycle and rode home into the glory of the evening. Even the cricket match was forgotten for a little while as he looked at the blaze of colour which celebrated the close of the day. He rode slowly, lingering as at a majestic rite. The whole vast sky glowed red and orange; the trees shone rosy in the reflected light which touched the hills. No breath of wind stirred the glowing stillness. His heart worshipped God and colour and life.

And night was treading softly from the woods where the little owls were beginning to cry.

In the Square the band gradually assembled and put on their instruments and began to play. For miles around their music carried; and so clear and so still was the air of the evening that farmers on the hills coming from their stables stood still for a moment and remarked: 'Ah! there's the band then! Hear it plain to-night,' and they were answered, after a listening pause:

'Yes, there's the band. You're right. Hear it plain too.'

People from all the villages round walked in little groups to Tillingfold to shop and drink and gossip. They stood thickly about in the main street, making reluctant room for the motors which every Saturday throughout the summer seemed to pass through the village in greater numbers.

Jim Saddler and Sam Bird edged carefully about in the crowd to collect two others for a quiet game of solo in the Village Room. Old Francis, who had declined John's invitation, they got for one, and deciding to pick up their fourth in the room, they set off down the street just as the band began to play its last piece. They saw Sid ahead of them who was pushing the pram, packed, somehow, with both tired little boys, and the sleeping baby.

'Rather him than me!' said Sam Bird, mysteriously. They passed Teddie White, properly stiff and uncomfortable in best suit and boots, on his way to the jollification – with his wife – his wife not quite walking with him, whether owing to her modesty or his, being uncertain.

Just about the time that Sid reached home after a morning's work, an afternoon's strenuous game, and a mile's shove home of a heavy pram, very glad to sit down and take his boots off, Mrs. Cairie leaned out of the window and called out to Horace, who had made his father come out on to the lawn and bowl at a stump with him, that she insisted upon his coming to bed *at once*, and Mrs. Trine patted her son Edgar's face as she left him to smoke a cigar with his father and two visiting men after dinner, saying how glad she was that he had had a nice game, and begging him not to let the gentlemen sit too long before joining the ladies – a ceremony which the Trines liked to maintain, though all the ladies smoked.

At this time, too, Dick Fanshawe climbed on to his bicycle to go and discuss the game with his friend, Paul Gauvinier – with life and art and morals thrown in, of course.

At length the band stopped playing and dispersed, the gossiping groups broke up and straggled away, some singing uproarious catches along the still lanes. Slowly the square emptied, the colour went out of the sky, and night descended peacefully upon the village of Tillingfold.

Rich and poor, old and young, were seeking sleep.